THE
VIRTUES
of a
STRONG SPIRIT

GLENN AREKION

Faith House Publishing

ISBN 978-1-943282-05-0

faithhousepublishing.com

Unless otherwise marked, all Scripture quotations are taken from the King James Version of the Bible.

Scripture quotations marked (NLT) are taken from the Holy Bible, New Living Translation, copyright © 1996, 2004, 2007 by Tyndale House Foundation. Used by permission of Tyndale House Publishers, Inc., Carol Stream, Illinois 60188. All rights reserved.

Scripture quotations marked (JUB) are taken from The Jubilee Bible, copyright © 2000, 2001, 2010 by Life Sentence Publishing, Aneko Press, from the Scriptures of the Reformation, edited by Russell M. Stendal. All rights reserved. Used by permission.

Scripture quotations marked (TLB) are taken from The Living Bible, copyright © 1971. Used by permission of Tyndale House Publishers, Inc., Carol Stream, Illinois 60188. All rights reserved.

Scripture quotations marked (NASB) are taken from the New American Standard Bible®, copyright © 1960, 1962, 1963, 1968, 1971, 1972, 1973, 1975, 1977, 1995 by The Lockman Foundation. Used by permission of Lockman.org.

Scripture quotations marked (AMP) are taken from the Amplified® Bible, copyright © 1954, 1958, 1962, 1964, 1965, 1987 by The Lockman Foundation. Used by permission of Lockman.org.

Scripture quotations marked (NIV) are taken from The Holy Bible, New International Version®, NIV®, copyright © 1973, 1978, 1984, 2011 by Biblica, Inc.™ Used by permission. All rights reserved worldwide.

Scripture quotations marked (WNT) are taken from The Weymouth New Testament, also known as The New Testament in Modern Speech or The Modern Speech New Testament. A translation from the text of The Resultant Greek Testament by Richard Francis Weymouth first published in 1903. In the public domain.

Scripture quotations marked (ISV) are taken from the Holy Bible: International Standard Version®. Copyright © 1996–forever by The ISV Foundation. All rights reserved internationally. Used by permission.

Scripture quotations marked (ARAM) are taken from The Original Aramaic New Testament in Plain English. Translated by Rev. Glenn David Bauscher. Copyright © 2012 Glenn David Bauscher. Used by permission.

Scripture quotations marked (NET Bible) are from the NET Bible®, copyright © 1996-2006 by Biblical Studies Press, L.L.C. Netbible.com. All rights reserved. Used by permission.

Scripture quotations marked (NCV) are from the New Century Version®, copyright © 2005 by Thomas Nelson, Inc. Used by permission. All rights reserved.

Further definitions taken from The NIV Theological Dictionary of New Testament Words (Zondervan Publishing House), W. E Vine's Expository Of New Testament Words, Adam's Clarke Commentary, Pulpit's Commentary

Printed in the United States of America

CONTENTS

CHAPTER 1
BE STRONG IN THE LORD

Finally, my brethren, be strong in the Lord, and in the power of his might.
(EPHESIANS 6:10)

THE great apostle Paul bluntly told us to be strong in the Lord. This was not a suggestion or an option but a mandate. He did not say to think and pray about it but that we simply must be strong in the Lord. The reason is because we are in a wrestling match: '*For we wrestle not against flesh and blood, but against principalities, against powers, against the rulers of the darkness of this world, against spiritual wickedness in high places.*' (Ephesians 6:12). Whether you like it or not, you must come to the realization that the world is a ring where you are engaged in a fight with a deadly enemy whose sole obsession is to destroy and get rid of you. He does not care how or when: his objective is your elimination from the game of life.

Peter gave us a clear picture of the intent of our enemy, '*Be sober, be vigilant; because your adversary the devil, as a roaring lion, walketh about, seeking whom he may devour.*' (1 Peter 5:8). He is looking for those that he can devour! In fact in Satan's mind, this is the game of death. The quicker you realize that you are in a wrestling match and at war, the quicker you will want to be equipped and strengthened. I once read a quote on war from Dwight D Eisenhower that pretty much sums up what our mindset must be:

'War is a terrible thing. But if you're going to get into it, you've got to get into it all the way.'

There was a time where our adversary had the upper hand over us. After the fall of the first man, Adam, and up till the Last Adam (Jesus), Satan wreaked havoc on the human race.

The Lord Jesus himself said:

*...your father **the devil**, and the lusts of your father ye will do. **He was a murderer from the beginning**...*

JOHN 8:44

The devil's administration or regime is one of murder, robbery, destruction and death (John 10:10). In fact King Solomon sheds some light on our predicament:

*So I returned, and considered all the **oppressions** that are done under the sun: and behold the tears of such as were **oppressed**, and they had no comforter; and on the side of their **oppressors** there was power; but they had no comforter. Wherefore I praised the dead which are already dead more than the living which are yet alive. Yea, better is he than both they, which hath not yet been, who hath not seen the evil work that is done under the sun.*

ECCLESIASTES 4:1-3

Here are three things that Solomon noticed that I have highlighted and want you to be aware of:

1. '**Oppressions** done under the sun'
2. 'Tears of the **Oppressed**'
3. 'On the side of the **Oppressor** there was power', is literally translated as 'power in the hand of the oppressor'. According to Bible Commentaries, it also reads, 'in and at the hand of the enemy, there was violence and power to crush.'

According to Peter, the oppressor is the devil (Acts 10:38) and there was a time when he had power in his hands to vex humanity, who became the oppressed. The power which he had enabled him to unleash oppression and violence under the sun on all human beings. In the beginning this was not the case, but from the fall of Adam, all of humanity were oppressed to the point of tears because there was no power to counteract Satan's power.

'War is a terrible thing. But if you're going to get into it, you've got to get into it all the way.' – Dwight D Eisenhower

---

Solomon surveyed the tussle between Satan and man's history and came to the conclusion that it was better off to be dead than to be alive. He went as far as to say that it would have been better off never to have been born. Why? Because if you were born, you would have to die, but before your death you would have had a full frontal encounter with the oppressor. Every person born in the earth after the fall was under the spell and jurisdiction of the enemy's power. Solomon construed that mankind was in an untenable position because our enemy had power on his side (literally in his hand) and we had no comforter (referring to Jesus and the Holy Spirit). Jesus said to the disciples, *'I will pray the Father and he shall give you another comforter...'* (John 14:16) meaning that He Himself was a comforter while He was with them and that they would receive another comforter, the Holy Spirit, after He goes back to heaven physically. No one in the Old Testament – after the fall of Adam – had the permanent indwelling residence of the Holy Spirit. It is noteworthy that the King James Version employed the word 'Comforter'. In Latin it is the word 'comfortis', a compound of 'com' meaning 'with' and 'fortis' meaning 'strength, support, help and force'. *Comfortis* would mean that the Holy Spirit comes with *help, strength* and *force*. In the middle of the 17th Century the word came to have the sense of 'something producing physical ease'. After the fall of Adam and prior to the coming of Jesus, man was doomed to dis-ability, dis-ease, distress, discouragement and disaster. Solomon became fully aware of three things:

❖ The oppressions done under the sun
❖ The tears of the oppressed
❖ Power in the hand of the oppressor

♂ Where did Satan get power to oppress humanity?

It was power in the hand of the oppressor (Satan) that inflicted oppressions upon people that caused them to have tears in their eyes. These oppressions came in different manifestations. Here is the dilemma! Where did Satan get the power in his hand to use against mankind? We know that after Lucifer fell, he had no power. Therefore he did not get this power to oppress from God. We know that after he rose up against God and fell he was stripped of his authority and power. Therefore after his fall (and prior to the fall of Adam), Satan was on the outside looking in with no power. Adam, on the other hand, was created with words of dominion, authority and power (Genesis 1:26-28). Some people have the idea that Adam was not aware of an enemy and that both he and Eve were caught by surprise by the devil. That is not the case!

After Lucifer fell and was cast out, he had no power but was on the outside looking in

---

*And God said, Let us make man in our image, after our likeness: and let them have **dominion** over the fish of the sea, and over the fowl of the air, and over the cattle, and over all the earth, and over every creeping thing that creepeth upon the earth. So God created man in his own image, in the image of God created he him; male and female created he them. And God blessed them, and God said unto them, Be fruitful, and multiply, and replenish the earth, and **subdue** it: and have dominion over the fish of the sea, and over the fowl of the air, and over every living thing that moveth upon the earth.*

GENESIS 1:26-28

The word 'subdue' in Hebrew is *kabash* and it means 'to make subject, tread down, make subservient, to trample under feet'

*And the Lord God took the man, and put him into the garden of Eden to dress it and to **keep** it.*

GENESIS 2:15

The word 'keep' in Hebrew is *shamar* and it means 'to be a watchman, to guard, to force and to protect its bounds'. These two Hebrew words clearly reveal to us that God had forewarned Adam of an intruding enemy who would seek to cross borders, but that Adam must be a watchman to protect his boundaries by trampling the intruder under his feet, making him subservient and subject to him.

Adam had all the authority, power, force and dominion: he was to protect his borders. However he failed and fell. Notice what God did after Adam did not enforce his authority to keep the Garden:

> *So he drove out the man; and he placed at **the east of the garden of Eden Cherubims, and a flaming sword which turned every way to KEEP the way of the tree of life.***
>
> GENESIS 3:24

Adam was to guard the garden and protect its boundaries but he did not. So God had cherubims to do exactly what Adam had failed to. Notice the cherubims had 'a flaming sword which turned every way to *keep* the way of the tree of life'. It is the same Hebrew word *shamar*. Adam had the same weapon – which was his tongue – as a sword to turn every way but he stayed silent and relinquished his dominion. The same Adam – who called God's creation from his rib 'woman' and named all the animals – was silent when the serpent was having a conversation with his wife, and relinquished his dominion. Silence was the relinquishing of his dominion. Now see what Satan told Jesus on the Mount of Temptations:

> *And the devil, taking him up into an high mountain, shewed unto him all the kingdoms of the world in a moment of time. And the devil said unto him, **All this power will I give thee, and the glory of them: for that is delivered unto me;** and to whomsoever I will I give it.*
>
> LUKE 4:5-6

> *And the devil said to Him, "I will give You **all this domain** and its glory; for it has been **handed over to me,** and I give it to whomever I wish.*
>
> NASB

*I will give You **authority over all** these kingdoms and all their glory, he said. **For it has been relinquished to me**, and I can give it to whom I wish.*
BEREAN STUDY BIBLE

Silence was the relinquishing and ceding of his dominion

⸷ Power Switch

Pay attention to the words, 'All this power will I give thee... for that is delivered to me.' As we can note from the other translations, 'handed and relinquished', Adam through high treason relinquished his authority, power, force and dominion to his chief enemy, Satan: power had switched hands and Satan began using the same dominion, power, force and authority of man *against* man. That which was supposed to be an effective and deadly weapon by Adam against Satan was now being used by Satan against Adam and his generations. The oppressions were brutal and relentless causing tears of sorrow, pain and powerlessness. The very weapons to protect Adam's boundaries were now being used as weapons of mass destruction upon the Adamic race. No wonder Solomon said, it was better off to be dead and even better never to have been born.

After the fall, power switched hands and man's own power was used to oppress and keep him in bondage

---

Because of the sin nature, that was passed on to every person born in the earth – due to Adam's transgression, mankind became subject to the abject reign of death of the devil.

Wherefore, as by one man sin entered into the world, and death by sin; and so death passed upon all men, for that all have sinned... For if by one man's offence death reigned by one... Therefore as by the offence of one judgment came upon all men to condemnation...
ROMANS 5:12, 17, 18

Solomon's fear was further amplified when he realized that there was no comforter on our side and in the hand of the enemy was power. Job also had the same assessment when he was going through great trials. He felt the need for a mediator and comforter:

Neither is there any daysman betwixt us, that might lay his hand upon us both.

JOB 9:33

The word *daysman* means 'an arbiter and umpire'. The story of Job teaches us that under the old economy, no matter how much you loved and served God, man was still subject to the devil because man did not have the permanent residency of the Spirit that became a reality through the all-sufficing blood sacrifice of Jesus, on Calvary's Cross. Hence the chagrin of Solomon! But if Solomon was alive today, he would be humming a different tune. Jesus said, '*and I will pray the Father, and He shall give you another comforter that He may abide with you forever.*' (John14:16). The Greek word used for *another comforter* is 'allos parakletos'.

The word *allos* means 'one of the same or exact kind and character' while *parakletos* means 'one sent alongside you to help and assist you.' The Amplified Bible gives us a sevenfold definition of *parakletos* as advocate, comforter, counselor, helper, intercessor, strengthener, and standby! While He was with His disciples, Jesus was a comforter to them but He told them that it was better for Him to go. Can you imagine how flabbergasted the disciples would have been? However, Jesus knew that in His physicality that He took on He could only be with them in one place but He wanted us to have the same exact kind of comfort abiding and dwelling in us permanently wherever we went. When Jesus ascended to heaven, the Holy Spirit came to take His place. The Holy Spirit is to us and in us today what Jesus would have been if He were still physically present on earth. So today we are no longer comfortless because of two things:

1 JESUS STRIPPED THE DEVIL OF HIS POWER THROUGH THE CROSS AND RESURRECTION

The Cross was a masterpiece plan of God designed before the foundation of the world. If Satan and his cohorts knew of this plan they would have never crucified Him:

*But we speak the wisdom of God in a mystery, even the hidden wisdom, which **God ordained before the world** unto our glory: **Which none of the princes of this world knew: for had they known it, they would not have crucified the Lord of glory.***

1 CORINTHIANS 2:7-8

*Forasmuch then as the children are partakers of flesh and blood, he also himself likewise took part of the same; **that through death he might destroy him that had the power of death, that is, the devil.***

HEBREWS 2:14

Calvary was a masterstroke act of the Godhead, to strip Satan of the authority of darkness and the power of death.

2 BECAUSE OF THE GENIUS OF REDEMPTION, WE ARE NOW INDWELT BY THE HOLY SPIRIT

*But ye are not in the flesh, but in the Spirit, if so be that **the Spirit of God dwell in you.** Now if any man have not the Spirit of Christ, he is none of his...But if the **Spirit of him that raised up Jesus from the dead dwell in you,** he that raised up Christ from the dead shall also quicken your mortal bodies by **his Spirit that dwelleth in you.***

ROMANS 8:9-11

*And I will pray the Father, and he shall give you another Comforter, that he may abide with you for ever; Even the Spirit of truth; whom the world cannot receive, because it seeth him not, neither knoweth him: but ye know him; **for he dwelleth with you, and shall be in you.***

JOHN 14:16-17

Now, having become a recipient of redemption does not mean that the devil will not attack you. He is still on the attack but this time we have authority and power to stop him just like Jesus stopped him in His earthly ministry. The ministry of Jesus upon the earth is a reflection of the life of the born-again believer. However we must be strong! Over and over we are told in the Scriptures to be strong. Joshua was told to be strong in order to take the people into their inheritance (Joshua 1:6, 7, 9). So What does it mean to be strong? To be strong in the Lord is:

- ❖ To be strong in faith
- ❖ To be strong in the Word
- ❖ To be strong in hope
- ❖ To be strong in grace
- ❖ To be strong in your spirit

Real strength is in your spirit man, your inner man that will enable and empower your outer man to deal with life's many challenging circumstances. It is your personal responsibility to develop your spirit. Just as you take the time to feed, exercise and look after your body, you need to give as much time to your spirit man. In the following pages, we will look at the virtues of developing a strong spirit.

The Cross was a masterpiece plan of God
designed before the foundation of the world

CHAPTER 2
UNDERSTANDING THE HUMAN SPIRIT

And the very God of peace sanctify you wholly; and I pray God your whole spirit and soul and body be preserved blameless unto the coming of our Lord Jesus Christ.

1 THESSALONIANS 5:23

IF you have been born again for some time, by now you must realize that man is a tripartite being consisting of spirit, soul and body. If you have read the writings of Paul, this is very evident for us to see. So, to drill it into your mind you must understand that man is a spirit, he has a soul which is made up of his mind, will and emotions, and he lives in a physical body. This is the make up of the whole man.

According to the apostle Paul this tripartite being – yet one person – can be summed up as the inward man and the outward man. The inward man is made up of your spirit and your soul whereas the outward man is the body of flesh that we see. James in his epistle wrote, '*For as the body without the spirit is dead, so faith without works is dead also.*' (James 2:26). Your body or the outward man needs your inward man to live but your inward man does not need your outward to live. Job notified us of this fact in his book, '*But there is **a spirit in man**: and the inspiration of the Almighty giveth them understanding.*' (Job 32:8). Peter, in his writing called the inward man the hidden man of the heart. It is called hidden man because we do not see the spirit but the body:

"*But let it be the **hidden man of the heart**, in that which is not corruptible, even the ornament of a meek and quiet **spirit**, which is in the sight of God of great price.*"

1 PETER 3:4

*For he is not a Jew, which is one outwardly; neither is that circumcision, which is outward in the flesh: But he is a Jew, which is one inwardly; and circumcision is that of **the heart, in the spirit**, and not in the letter; whose praise is not of men, but of God.*

ROMANS 2:28-29

Paul was informing us here that the spirit is the heart. It was the spirit man that was made in the image of God: God took the earth to fashion the body in the image of the man.

*And God said, Let us make man **in our image**, after **our likeness**: and let them have dominion over the fish of the sea, and over the fowl of the air, and over the cattle, and over all the earth, and over every creeping thing that creepeth upon the earth.*

GENESIS 1:26

◌ The Spirit of Man

The Word explains that man was made in the image and likeness of God. The word 'man' is a generic term for mankind or humanity comprising of male and female. We have the male species man, and the 'wo-man' who is the man species with the womb.

Jesus himself said that God is a Spirit (John 4:24). If anyone was and is an authority figure on this subject and could define God it would be Jesus, as He himself is God and from eternity past has been with the Father in the Godhead. God is a Spirit! In fact Moses and the writer of Hebrews unfold this great truth:

*And Moses spake unto the Lord, saying, Let the Lord, **the God of the spirits of all flesh**...*

NUMBERS 27:15-16

*Furthermore we have had fathers of our flesh which corrected us, and we gave them reverence: shall we not much rather be in subjection unto the **Father of spirits**, and live?*

HEBREWS 12:9

This denotes that man is primarily a spirit and not just a body of flesh and blood. Within every living human body there is a human spirit. This is the real person, the one created in the image of God. Your spirit man is the real man and your body is the sheath or the suit that covers it. Your body looks like your spirit. Your body features look the way they do right now because your skeletal make up and flesh has enveloped the structure of your spirit man. So when people ask, 'Are we going to know each other in heaven?' The answer is simple! If you know me now, you will know me in heaven and if you don't know me now you will get to know me in heaven. Remember the story that Jesus told about the rich man and Lazarus (Luke 16:20-31)?After both of them died, the rich man recognized and remembered Lazarus. Why? Because the spirit structure of Lazarus looked exactly the same as before except he did not have any sores or sicknesses.

> *But there is a spirit in man: and the inspiration of the Almighty giveth them understanding.*
>
> JOB 32:8

Way before the writings of Paul, Job established the teachings of both Paul and Jesus and it is through the spirit of man that God wants to establish communication. After the fall of Adam man had to learn things from his sensory mechanisms due to the fact that his spirit was separated from God. Everything we learn comes through the senses and the soul realm: the intellectual realm. Our education is grounded in the sense and intellectual realm. However since God is the father of spirits and we are spirit beings then His primary way to communicate with us will be through our spirits. The new creation is the born again spirit man.

The spirit man was created in the image of God then God took the dust of the ground to fashion the body in the image of the spirit man

---

So keep this in your thinking, 'You are a spirit, you have a soul and you live in a physical body.' Your body is your earthly suit that covers your spirit man but it is not the real you. The real you is the spirit man. This is why Paul said, *'flesh and blood cannot inherit the Kingdom of God'* (1 Corinthians 15:50). As a matter of fact the spirit man will live on after the body has expired. The spirit man – which is the real you – will leave the body after death and either head for heaven or hell. If one is born again and washed in the blood of Jesus then the spirit man goes to heaven and if one is not born again then the spirit man goes to hell. Your body is simply the sheath of your spirit. This truth bears out in the book of Daniel:

> *"I Daniel was grieved in **my spirit** in the midst of **my body**, and the visions of my head troubled me."*

DANIEL 7:15

The Aramaic word for body is *nidneh* נִדְנֶה and it means a sheath, a receptacle. Adam Clarke's Commentary on this verse is very enlightening:

'I Daniel was grieved, etc. – The words in the original are uncommonly emphatic. My spirit was grieved, or sickened, הנדנ וגב bego nidneh, within its sheath or scabbard. Which I think proves:

1. That the human spirit is different from the body.

2. That it has a proper subsistence independently of the body, which is only its sheath for a certain time.

3. That the spirit may exist independently of its body, as the sword does independently of its sheath.'

CLARKE'S COMMENTARY

The word 'man' is a generic term for mankind
or humanity, comprising of male and female

Here are some other remarks that Paul made:

...to be absent from the body is to be present with the Lord.

2 CORINTHIANS 5:8

*For I am in a strait betwixt two, having **a desire to depart**, and to be with Christ; which is far better: Nevertheless to **abide in the flesh** is more needful for you.*

PHILIPPIANS 1:23-24

These are specific references to the fact that at death – the time of physical expiration – the spirit man vacates the body of flesh and heads for its eternal destination. Please note that Paul employed the words 'to depart'. Therefore as James said, *'For as the body without the spirit is dead...'* (James 2:26) you need to realize that your body needs your spirit but your spirit does not need your body. Your spirit only needs your body to make you legal on the earth and to function on the earth. God designed for man's spirit to be the king of his triune personality, with the soul and body under obedience.

Therefore you need to be ever conscious that you are a spirit. We live in a world where we are over conscious of our bodies and little time is given to the spirit man even within the church world. Here's what you really need to know in a nutshell:

❖ With my spirit, I connect with God – my spirit is recreated and saved;
❖ With my soul, I connect on an intellectual and emotional level – my mind needs renewing by the Word and is being saved gradually;
❖ With my body, I connect to the physical world – my body needs to be subject to my inner man by the Word and it will be saved when I receive a glorified body.

Some people and even ministers have confused the soul and spirit: they think that they are the same, but the Bible teaches us differently. Sometimes you will hear ministers say, 'It was a great service and sixty souls were saved.' What they mean by that is that sixty persons accepted Jesus Christ as their Savior. While this is fine and we understand the terminology, the bible makes it clear that there is a distinction between the soul and the spirit. Although they are closely knit in that they make up the inner man, the Scripture says there is a divisible line between them that only the Word can maneuver:

> *For the word of God is quick, and powerful, and sharper than any two-edged sword, piercing even to the dividing asunder of soul and spirit...*
> HEBREWS 4:12

If they were same, they could not be divided. The soul of man is comprised of the mind, the will, the emotions and the intellect. The soul is the operating system for information, learning, logic and reason, acting like a hard drive on a computer, only that it is alive and attached to the life center – your spirit.

The body is the tent, the tabernacle, the dwelling place, the sheath and the vehicle of expression for the spirit and soul. The body is the outward man, the physical, the house in which our inward man resides. Paul also said to the Corinthians, '*For which cause we faint not; but though our outward man perish, yet the inward man is renewed day by day.*' (2 Corinthians 4:16). The outward man – the body – is decaying and getting older by the day but your inward man – your spirit – is renewed on a daily basis. Paul also called our body the earthly house:

> *For we know that if our earthly house of this tabernacle were dissolved, we have a building of God, an house not made with hands, eternal in the heavens.*
> 2 CORINTHIANS 5:1

The earthly house of this tabernacle is the body but even when this house is dissolved we still have a house not made with hands: the spirit which came from the breath and word of God and will live eternally. One day I will have a new body, a glorified body. In the meantime I have new life, the zoe-life of God in my spirit, in my inward man.

CHAPTER 3
THE FUNCTIONS OF THE SPIRIT MAN

In this chapter I will give you four basic functions of your spirit man.There are more but these four will be fundamental to your success.

*My son, attend to my words; incline thine ear unto my sayings. Let them not depart from thine eyes; keep them in the midst of thine heart. For they are life unto those that find them, and health to all their flesh. **Keep thy heart with all diligence; for out of it are the issues of life.***

PROVERBS 4:20-23

Firstly, understand that when the bible uses the word 'heart', it is not referring to the flesh organ that pumps blood but it is used interchangeably with the spirit of man. Both Peter and Paul used the word 'heart' to refer to the spirit of man.:

*But let it be the **hidden man of the heart**, in that which is not corruptible, even the ornament of a meek and quiet **spirit**, which is in the sight of God of great price.*

1 PETER 3:4

*For he is not a Jew, which is one outwardly; neither is that circumcision, which is outward in the flesh: But he is a Jew, which is one **inwardly**; and circumcision is that of **the heart, in the spirit**, and not in the letter; whose praise is not of men, but of God.*

ROMANS 2:28-29

And the Lord direct your hearts...

2 THESSALONIANS 3:5

Just as your physical heart is the life source and pumps blood to the rest of the body, your spirit man is the life source of your being and this is why Solomon told us to protect, with all vigilance, our heart/spirit because out of it are the issues of life (Proverbs 4:23). The Hebrew word for 'issues' is **towtsa'ah** תּוֹצָאוֹת and it means:

❖ Outgoing
❖ Border
❖ A going out
❖ Extremity
❖ Source of life
❖ Escape
❖ Deliverance
❖ Forces of life
❖ Geographical boundary.

Different translations of this verse give a much better comprehension:

Above all else, guard your heart, for everything you do flows from it.
NIV

Guard your heart above all else, for it determines the course of your life.
NLT

Keep your heart with all vigilance, for from it flow the springs of life.
ESV

Guard your heart above all else, for it is the source of life.
HCSB

Guard your heart with all vigilance, for from it are the sources of life.
NET

Keep your heart with all caution because from it is the outgoing of life.
ARAMAIC BIBLE IN PLAIN ENGLISH

The Pulpit Commentary expounds on this verse as such: '*Keep thy heart with all diligence; properly, **above all things that have to be guarded, keep or guard thy heart**.*' So we can clearly see that it is our responsibility to vigilantly protect our spirit because it determines the boundaries of our lives. The forces of life – meaning the nine fruit of the Spirit – flow from your inward man and according to Paul, '*against such there is no law*' (Galatians 5:23) meaning they make you unstoppable.

Limitless boundaries

THE FIRST THING to realize about your spirit man is that it sets the boundaries of your life and from it flow the forces of life – the nine fruit of the Spirit – to make you unbeatable. How far you want to go in life and how big you want to be in life is determined by the conditioning of your spirit. Your escape, health and deliverance are largely determined by the condition of your spirit. When your spirit is properly conditioned, it does not matter where you find yourself, you can grow out of it. This means no-one can limit you but yourself. Remember, the Holy Spirit is abiding in your human spirit, therefore because of Him you are limitless. You can go anywhere from where you are right now because of the Holy Spirit in your spirit.

The abiding and indwelling Holy Spirit within your spirit makes you limitless

---

Base of power and operation

SECONDLY, the spirit man is the base of power, authority and dominion:

> *And God said, Let us make man in our image, after our likeness: and let them have dominion over the fish of the sea, and over the fowl of the air, and over the cattle, and over all the earth, and over every creeping thing that creepeth upon the earth.*
>
> GENESIS 1:26

Remember that God fashioned the body of man in Genesis 2:7, '*And the Lord God formed man of the dust of the ground, and breathed into his nostrils the breath of life; and man became a living soul.*' Therefore when God was speaking words of dominion in the creation of man in Genesis 1:26, He was speaking to the spirit. Hence authority, power and dominion were directed to the spirit of man. Adam was supposed to dominate the outside from the inside, control the outer from the inner and rule the physical from the spiritual. The same applies today, as you go through your Christian life, you dominate and rule the exterior from the base of your spirit. Paul said to the Roman believers that he '*serves God with his spirit*' (Romans 1:9). To enjoy the fruit of Christianity your base of operation must be your spirit. This is why Paul told us:

> ...*the righteousness of the law might be fulfilled in us, **who walk not after the flesh, but after the Spirit**. For they that are after the flesh do mind the things of the flesh; but they that are after the Spirit the things of the Spirit. For to be carnally minded is death; but to be spiritually minded is life and peace.*
>
> ROMANS 8:4-6

> *This I say then, Walk in the Spirit, and ye shall not fulfil the lust of the flesh. For the flesh lusteth against the Spirit, and the Spirit against the flesh: and these are contrary the one to the other: so that ye cannot do the things that ye would.*
>
> GALATIANS 5:16-17

As you can see from the Authorized Version the word 'Spirit' has a capital 's' conveying the idea of the Holy Spirit, but that could not be so as the Holy Spirit does not lust against the flesh. This is referring to *your* spirit man who wants the ascendency over your flesh. Of course your spirit has desires to do good because of the indwelling Holy Spirit. My point is that we must operate from the base of our spirit, living from the inside out as God always meant for us to live.

The lamp that shines and guides

THIRDLY, Solomon sheds more light as it pertains to the function of our spirit man:

> *The spirit of man is the candle of the Lord, searching all the inward parts of the belly.*
>
> PROVERBS 20:27

Newer translations employ the word 'lamp' and so it would read as, '*The spirit of man is the **lamp** of the Lord, searching all the inward parts of the belly.*' This is simply informing us that God will guide us via our spirit man. This is why I keep saying over and over just to drill it into your thinking:

* With your spirit, you connect with God and the things of the Spirit;
* With your soul, you connect with the mental, intellectual and emotional world;
* With your body, you connect with the physical world.

Apart from the Word of God, which directs and gives us the general will of God, the other predominant way that God guides the New Testament believer is through his spirit. Now because many believers have not developed this skill, they resort to physical things such as fleecing as a form of guidance. 'Putting out a fleece', as it is often expressed, involves seeking God's will or direction through a sign. For example someone says, "Lord, if this is really you then let me run into so and so, or for my phone to ring three times or, let a red truck pass in front of me." As absurd as this sounds there are untold millions of believers who live their lives from this prescription. That is not how God intended for us to live and it is not God's best! Many have fallen into this trap and Satan can easily deceive and destroy people with fleeces. Some have retorted, "If it was good enough for Gideon, it is good enough for me." Let's look a little closer at that.

The notion of the 'fleece' is based on Gideon who was one of the leaders that God raised up to deliver Israel from the Midianites. The Angel of the Lord appeared to him and gave him specific instructions. But before Gideon would commit himself to battle, he wanted to make sure that God was going to give Israel the victory and he started his fleecings:

> *Gideon said to God, 'If you will save Israel by my hand as you have promised – look, I will place a wool fleece on the threshing floor. If there is dew only on the fleece and all the ground is dry, then I will know that you will save Israel by my hand, as you said.' And that is what happened. Gideon rose early the next day; he squeezed the fleece and wrung out the dew – a bowlful of water. Then Gideon said to God, 'Do not be angry with me. Let me make just one more request. Allow me one more test with the fleece, but this time make the fleece dry and let the ground be covered with dew.' That night God did so. Only the fleece was dry; all the ground was covered with dew.*
>
> JUDGES 6:36-40 NIV

I am going to include an excerpt from my book 'Receiving direction from above' which will give you more detailed information about hearing God's voice. Here's the excerpt:

There are two things to note as we probe into this event:

❖ Firstly, Gideon did not put the fleece in order to discover the will of God. He already knew that from the angel who specifically told him what must transpire. Gideon knew what God wanted him to do, nevertheless he went ahead with this fleece.

❖ Secondly, the fleece was a sign of unbelief. The Lord Jesus himself had some strong words for those who ask for signs: '*Then certain of the scribes and of the Pharisees answered, saying, Master, we would see a sign from thee. But he answered and said unto them, An evil and adulterous generation seeketh after a sign; and there shall no sign be given to it, but the sign of the prophet Jonas*' (Matthew 12:38, 39).

Asking for signs, typifies today's believers who walk by sight rather than walking by faith. Gideon had already received a miraculous sign from God pointing him to victory and deliverance for Israel. Nevertheless Gideon doubted; even after the angel of the Lord appeared to him, he wanted one sign after another. Gideon knew God's will but didn't believe it. 'Putting out a fleece' was an act of faith*less*ness because Gideon didn't trust that God would do what He had already promised. He wanted more signs when an angel speaking to him should have been enough of a sign already. Jesus told us, '*Blessed are they that have not seen, and yet have believed.*' (John 20:29). Many years ago, Kenneth Hagin taught the church world, "Fleeces are an Old Covenant method of guidance used by spiritually dead people. We have a better guide, the living Spirit of God in direct communion with our spirit." You are not spiritually dead but alive in Christ by the Holy Ghost. So let me say this categorically: **fleecing is not the way God wants to give you direction. You have to press into God in order to hear him.** Luke 5:1; "*And it came to pass, that, as the people pressed upon him to hear the word of God, he stood by the lake of Gennesaret...*" Allow me to re-emphasize this point in your mind. Although it is the birthright of every believer to receive direction from the mouth of God, it will not come cheaply nor with a flippant or nonchalant attitude. You must learn to press for his voice to direct your steps.

RECEIVING DIRECTION FROM ABOVE – GLENN AREKION

---

*Fleecing is not the New Testament way of guidance
for the believer. We are to be led by the voice
of the Spirit from our spirit*

You must grasp this truth. God will lead you from your spirit man which is the candle or lamp of the Lord. Paul said this to the Thessalonians: '*And the Lord direct your hearts...*' (2 Thessalonians 3:5). We know the heart is the spirit of man. See what King David says:

> For thou wilt **light my candle:** the Lord my God will enlighten my darkness. For by thee I have run through a troop; and by my God have I leaped over a wall.
>
> PSALM 18:28-29

God will light up his candle, meaning his spirit man, and shine the torch on the darkness he was experiencing that was proving to be a roadblock and obstruction. But once his spirit has been enlightened, he can run through a troop that have conspired to destroy him, and jump over any obstacle. This is what will happen to you when you pay attention to your spirit man and the inward witness. Now look at the words of the patriarch Job:

> Oh that I were as in months past, as in the days when **God preserved me; When his candle shined upon my head, and when by his light I walked through darkness;** As I was in the days of my youth, when the secret of God was upon my tabernacle; When the Almighty was yet with me, when my children were about me; When I washed my steps with butter, and the rock poured me out rivers of oil; When I went out to the gate through the city, when I prepared my seat in the street!
>
> JOB 29:2-7

Job reminisced about the time of divine protection when God guided him by his spirit. When the Lord guides you by your spirit, you will receive protection and prosperity. Solomon also told us that your spirit is searching all the inward parts of the belly. Your spirit is aware of things that your head is not, because of the indwelling Holy Spirit within your spirit. You need to trust the guidance of the Holy Spirit within your spirit man which many times will be expressed as an inward witness as Paul described: '*The Spirit itself beareth witness with our spirit...*' (Romans 8:16).

Sustainer and a support system in times of crisis

FOURTHLY, your spirit man is a sustainer to uphold you in times of crisis:

The spirit of a man will sustain his infirmity; but a wounded spirit who can bear?

PROVERBS 18:14

I want to look at this verse from different translations and then give you the most accurate rendering of this verse:

A healthy spirit conquers adversity, but what can you do when the spirit is crushed?

MESSAGE

The human spirit can endure a sick body, but who can bear a crushed spirit?

NLT

The strong spirit of a man sustains him in bodily pain or trouble, but a weak and broken spirit who can raise up or bear?

AMPLIFIED BIBLE

We can clearly see the effect of having a healthy spirit is that it sustains you during tough or sick times. The Amplified aptly puts it: '*The strong spirit of man... a weak and broken spirit.*' The choice is simple, you either have a strong or a weak spirit. You either have a healthy spirit or a crushed spirit. From my in-depth studies of this particular verse, allow me to give you a strong and accurate rending of this verse:

"A man's strong spirit endures and sustains him during tough and sick times but a weak and crushed spirit will be his demise."

GLENN AREKION

This is very serious! A weak and crushed spirit will be his demise. This is the consequence of a weak spirit. Another rendering of this verse is: '*A man's strong spirit will uphold him through any crisis but a crushed spirit will be his downfall.*' This is why it is our duty to protect our spirit man. Feed it the right food in order to keep it healthy and strong. The Apostle Paul was well aware of this truth and this is why he prayed for the Ephesian saints: '*That he would grant you, according to the riches of his glory, to be strengthened with might by his Spirit in the inner man.*' (Ephesians 3:16).

A strong spirit sustains, endures and conquers; a weak and crushed spirit will bring a tragic demise

---

Real strength is in the spirit man. There are things that we do that will strengthen the spirit man and there are things that we do that will vex and weaken our spirit. However if you protect your spirit with all vigilance, as Solomon declared, then out of it will flow the forces and issues of life that will sustain you in tough and sick times. Your spirit, when it is properly nurtured, will sustain you. Now let us look at the virtues of a strong spirit.

CHAPTER 4
THE VIRTUES OF A STRONG SPIRIT 1-4

If thou faint in the day of adversity, thy strength is small.

PROVERBS 24:10

If you fall to pieces in a crisis, there wasn't much to you in the first place.

MESSAGE

For which cause we faint not...

2 CORINTHIANS 4:16

MANY people are legends in their own mind; they think that they are strong but another reality shows up when they go through pressure and times of trouble. Everybody living on earth will have days of adversity but we do not have to cave in and fall apart like a cheap dollar clock when they show up.

He that hath knowledge spareth his words: and a man of understanding is of an excellent spirit.

PROVERBS 17:27

He that hath knowledge spareth his words; and a man of understanding is of a cool spirit.

DARBY

Be cool under pressure

Many would like to think that they are cool. So many work out in the gym to build a Mr Olympia body, only to fall to pieces when they go through a crisis. Looking like Mr Olympia and falling to pieces in a crisis is not cool.

The image does not add up. Some people think that they are cool because of how they dress or their hairstyle. But what is the point of wearing a $5,000 suit, but you cry, fret, have a tantrum and panic when pressure hits you? That is not cool!

The image of looking like Mr Olympia and falling to pieces in a crisis is not cool and does not add up

---

♪ Jesus

We have to learn to be like Jesus who, when the disciples were going through a mega storm, was sleeping in the hinder part of the ship on a pillow. While they were all falling apart, Jesus was cool under pressure because He had a strong spirit (Mark 5). We know He had strong spirit for the bible says:

> *And the child grew, and waxed strong in spirit, filled with wisdom: and the grace of God was upon him.*
>
> LUKE 2:40

♪ Peter

We need to be like Peter after the Resurrection, when he was arrested by Herod who had already decapitated James and had decreed a death sentence over his life. Herod planned to publicly execute Peter after Easter. The night before his execution, Peter was sleeping between two quaternions of soldiers who were chained to him. If that was the average person, they would not be sleeping ;Peter learned to be cool under pressure from the Master, Jesus. In fact Peter was so cool under pressure that he slept so heavily, the angel had to kick him to awake him for his deliverance. Peter was cool under pressure (Acts 12).

♪ Paul

We need to be like Paul who, when he was in a storm for fourteen days was cool enough not to panic but to hear from God. While everybody was throwing up and throwing away all their stuff to the point where even Dr. Luke said, *'All hope that we could be saved was then taken away'*, Paul told them to cheer up , *'for there shall be no loss of any man's life among you... Wherefore, sirs, be of good cheer: for I believe God, that it shall be even as it was told me.'* (Acts 27). Paul was very strong in his spirit even when he listed his persecutions and problems, he made a startling revelation:

> *'Are they ministers of Christ? (I speak as a fool) I am more; in labours more abundant, in stripes above measure, in prisons more frequent, in deaths oft. Of the Jews five times received I forty stripes save one. Thrice was I beaten with rods, once was I stoned, thrice I suffered shipwreck, a night and a day I have been in the deep; In journeyings often, in perils of waters, in perils of robbers, in perils by mine own countrymen, in perils by the heathen, in perils in the city, in perils in the wilderness, in perils in the sea, in perils among false brethren; In weariness and painfulness, in watchings often, in hunger and thirst, in fastings often, in cold and nakedness. Beside those things that are without, that which cometh upon me daily, the care of all the churches. **Who is weak, and I am not weak? who is offended, and I burn not? If I must needs glory, I will glory of the things which concern mine infirmities.***

2 CORINTHIANS 11:23-30

Only a man with a strong spirit can speak like this. See his words: *'For the which cause I also suffer these things: nevertheless I am not ashamed: **for I know whom I have believed, and am persuaded that he is able to keep that which I have committed unto him against that day.'*** (2 Timothy 1:12) and look what else he said: *'But **none of these things move me,** neither count I my life dear unto myself, so that I might finish my course with joy, and the ministry, which I have received of the Lord Jesus, to testify the gospel of the grace of God.'* (Acts 20:24).

There are many in the bible that had a very strong spirit and the list would be too long to mention them all here. The most important point is that we must make sure *we* have a strong spirit. While there are many more, I will give you twelve critical virtues of a strong spirit and expound upon them. In this chapter I will list four virtues of a strong spirit and in the following two chapters list the remaining eight. Then in the last several chapters I will show you how to train your spirit to be strong so you can go through any situation and win.

Virtue 1

A strong spirit is a sustainer and a conqueror that will uphold you through any given situation

*The spirit of a man **will sustain** his infirmity; but a wounded spirit who can bear?*

PROVERBS 18:14

*A healthy spirit **conquers adversity**, but what can you do when the spirit is crushed?*

MESSAGE

*The human spirit can **endure** a sick body, but who can bear a crushed spirit?*

NLT

*The strong spirit of a man **sustains** him in bodily pain or trouble, but a weak and broken spirit who can raise up or bear?*

AMPLIFIED BIBLE

A man's strong spirit endures and sustains him during tough and sick times but a weak and crushed spirit will be his demise.

DR GLENN AREKION

A great virtue of a strong spirit in a man is the capacity to go through anything. This covers the whole spectrum of problems. Not only will your strong spirit allow you to go through anything, but it will not bow, bend, burn or collapse. A strong spirit will conquer adversity. A strong spirit is like the lion, which has the spirit of a conqueror and will not retreat:

A lion which is strongest among beasts, and turneth not away for any.
                                                        PROVERBS 30:30

There is no problem that you are going through that can overwhelm you if have a strong spirit. When the Scripture tells you that you can go through anything, it means *anything*. A strong spirit does not say, 'I cannot take this any more!' or 'This is too much for me' or 'I'm at the end of my rope, I am done with this'. If you find yourself saying these words, it's an indication that your spirit is not as strong as you think it is. A strong spirit will look at the problem and tell it, 'If it's a fight you want, a fight is what you're going to get but when the dust settles, God and I will be standing on top.' Your spirit is a sustainer and a supporter of your body and your mental faculties. Your spirit will uphold you in trying times. God will light and lift you from your spirit by the Holy Spirit in you. Like David, you can say, '*Yea though I walk through the valley of the shadow of death, I will fear no evil.*' (Psalm 23:4). From today, make this your confession:

My spirit is healthy. My spirit is strong and it will sustain me through anything I am going through or will ever go through. My spirit is a sustainer. I am a conqueror in Christ. I cannot be defeated and I will not quit.

A strong spirit does not say, 'I cannot take this any more!'
or 'This is too much for me!'

Virtue 2

A strong spirit easily yields to God and his Word without argument, making the Logos to become the logic

A strong spirit person has understood and made the Word the first and final authority in their life. As Brother Hagin said many years ago, 'The Bible says it, that settles it whether you believe it or not.' Arguing and rationalizing the Word is doubt and unbelief in action. There are many so-called bible believers who argue with the Scripture. You will hear them say, 'Now I know the Bible says that **but...**' There is no **but**! If God says something, it is established; God's word is unchangeable and unbreakable. I like how the Message Translation informs us about Abraham's faith:

> *Abraham didn't focus on his own impotence and say, "It's hopeless. This hundred-year-old body could never father a child." Nor did he survey Sarah's decades of infertility and give up. **He didn't tiptoe around God's promise asking cautiously skeptical questions...***

ROMANS 4:19-21

⸉ Skeptical arguments

Too many people are in this boat of fighting and arguing with God. I like the way it says, '*Asking cautiously skeptical questions...*' Today we have believers and even ministers that say, 'Now brother, we have to be very careful. Just because you see something in the bible that does not mean it is for us today.'

Well, who in the world is it for then?

Yes, yes and a thousand times yes: if you see something in the bible then it is for you. You have a covenantal and redemptive legal right to it. If you are skeptical about God's promises then they won't manifest in your life. If you choose to be a *believing* believer then this will be the outcome: '*And blessed is she that believed: for there shall be a performance of those things which were told her from the Lord.*' (Luke 1:45). Stop arguing with God over what the devil and your circumstances are saying and argue with the devil and your circumstances over what God has already said. Stop telling God about your mountain and start talking to your mountain about God. You've got to become like Mary when she received the Word from Gabriel: '...*be it unto me according to thy word.*' (Luke 1:38).

Zacharias on the other hand asked a skeptical question arguing with God, and Gabriel had to close his mouth for a season. The question has to be asked, 'Why is it that both Zacharias and Mary asked a question and only Zacharias mouth was shut?'

ᛞ Zacharias' question

And Zacharias said unto the angel, Whereby shall I know this? for I am an old man, and my wife well stricken in years.

LUKE 1:18

ᛞ Mary's question

Then said Mary unto the angel, How shall this be, seeing I know not a man?

LUKE 1:34

Both asked a question but only Zacharias' mouth was shut. Why? Because Mary's question was biological and Zacharias' was skeptical. Mary knew enough about biology to understand that the method for a child to be born in this earth is through sexual intercourse. That is why she asked, '...*seeing I know not a man*', meaning I have not had sexual relation with a man. That's simple logic and Gabriel went on to explain how it would take place, '*The Holy Ghost shall come upon thee, and the power of the Highest shall overshadow thee: therefore also that holy thing which shall be born of thee shall be called the Son of God.*' (Luke 1:35).

Zacharias' question on the other hand was skeptical born out of unbelief. Look at how Gabriel greeted Zacharias, '*Fear not, Zacharias: for **thy prayer is heard;** and thy wife Elisabeth shall bear thee a son, and thou shalt call his name John.*' (Luke 1:13). The reason why his question was skeptical was because Gabriel appeared to him based upon **his prayer request**.

Mary's question was biological and Zacharias' was skeptical

Elizabeth had been barren but they were still praying for a child. When Gabriel appeared to him with the good news, Zacharias did not even believe in his own prayers and skeptically asked how this was going to take place seeing they were both advanced in years. Apparently Zacharias completely forgot about Abraham and Sarah. Elizabeth had been praying and all the people outside were praying but Zacharias, in the holy presence of God, was arguing – unbelievingly – with Gabriel! So the angel just shut his mouth for a season. The lesson to learn here is, 'Once you have prayed, if you cannot say anything faith filled don't abort the miracle: learn the vocabulary of silence.' Skepticism is the unfolding of unbelief. The point I want to drive into your spirit is that the Word is unbreakable; all of life and existence revolves around the integrity of one verse in the Bible:

> **God is not a man, that he should lie;** *neither the son of man, that he should repent: hath he said, and shall he not do it? or hath he spoken, and shall he not make it good?*
>
> NUMBERS 23:19

God is not a man that He should lie. The author of Hebrews tells us that it is impossible for God to lie (Hebrews 11:18). Paul also echoed the same sentiment in his letter to Titus when he wrote that God cannot lie (Titus 1:2). If your spirit is to be strong you must once and for all settle this truth in your heart. You cannot just mentally assent to the Word when your actions deny its reality.

When it comes to the Word, let this be the anchor in your mind:

Forever O Lord thy Word is settled in the heavens.

PSALM 119:89

The words of the Lord are pure words: as silver tried in a furnace of earth, purified seven times.

PSALM 12:6

The believer with a strong spirit is one whose mind is constantly being renewed with the Word. The renewing of the mind is simply making the Logos become your logic and when you get to that place nothing will shake you. This will be your reality:

*Praise ye the Lord. Blessed is the man that feareth the Lord, that **delighteth greatly in his commandments.** His seed shall be mighty upon earth: the generation of the upright shall be blessed. Wealth and riches shall be in his house: and his righteousness endureth for ever... **He shall not be afraid of evil tidings: his heart is fixed, trusting in the Lord. His heart is established, he shall not be afraid,** until he see his desire upon his enemies.*

PSALM 112:1-3, 7, 8

As a believer with a strong spirit who delights in the Word, you will not be afraid of bad news. Your heart will be fixed, established, trusting in the Lord to see you through to the other side. The opposite of this is not a pretty picture:

*And it was **told the house of David,** saying, Syria is confederate with Ephraim. **And his heart was moved, and the heart of his people, as the trees of the wood are moved with the wind.***

ISAIAH 7:2

When your heart moves as the trees are moved by the wind, it indicates a weak spirit. It indicates that your heart is not fixed and established upon the veracity of God's unchangeable Word. You have to come to the place where you argue with the devil and circumstances over what God has said rather than arguing with God over what the devil is saying.

Argue with the devil and circumstances over what God has said rather than arguing with God over what the devil is saying.

Virtue 3

A strong spirit gives you the power of resistance

Another virtue of a strong spirit is that it gives you the power to resist as James declares in his letter: '*Submit yourselves therefore to God. **Resist the devil, and he will flee from you**'* (James 4:7). It is the believer's duty to resist the devil. If you do not resist him, he will rule over you. You don't have to let the devil and life's circumstance steamroll over you, on the contrary, you can steamroll over the devil and his works! Peter also admonished us to resist the devil:

> *Be sober, be vigilant; because **your adversary the devil, as a roaring lion, walketh about, seeking whom he may devour: Whom resist stedfast in the faith,** knowing that the same afflictions are accomplished in your brethren that are in the world.*

> 1 PETER 5:8-9

Paul, in writing to the Ephesian saints boldly announced: '*Neither give place to the devil.*' (Ephesians 4:27). We know the word 'place' is the Greek word *topos* from which we get the word 'topography' referring to the measuring of the land. Paul was simply telling us not to give the devil an inch, centimeter or yard because if you do he will take much more than you have given him.

Remember, Paul fought the beasts of Ephesus and won:

If after the manner of men I have fought with beasts at Ephesus...

                                          1 CORINTHIANS 15:32

Paul took on the principalities and powers behind the religious leaders and won the victory. The devil *will* come against you and you must be prepared to resist him. Satan loves soft ground and if he finds you as soft ground then he will dig into you. He devours the person of least resistance; don't give him this privilege: resist him and he will flee from you. He went against Peter and Paul and he will certainly go against you but the good news is if you resist him he will flee from you. What do we need to resist?

ᔫ Resist the devil as he attempts to thwart your destiny.

He endeavored to hinder the life and ministry of Paul.

Wherefore we would have come unto you, even I Paul, once and again; but Satan hindered us.

                                      1 THESSALONIANS 2:18

For we wanted to come to you--certainly I, Paul, did, again and again – but Satan blocked our way.

                                      NIV

For we wanted to come to you--indeed I, Paul, tried again and again – but Satan obstructed us.

                                  BEREAN STUDY BIBLE

For we wanted to come to you (I, Paul, in fact tried again and again) but Satan thwarted us."

                                  NET BIBLE

If Satan obstructed and endeavored to thwart and obstruct the life of Paul, you can take it to the bank he will endeavor to thwart and obstruct you too. In fact one translation pens this verse with very strong language: '*We wanted to visit you. I, Paul, wanted to visit you twice already, but Satan made that impossible.*' (God's Word Translation). Right now you may feel that you should be further in life than you currently are. Why are you not in the place where you are supposed to be? For many, this is because, without their knowledge, the enemy has made it impossible. He would like for you to believe that *impossible progress* is your only option but that will only be the case if you do not resist him.

Now see what happened when Nehemiah was endeavoring to rebuild the walls of Jerusalem:

> *So built we the wall; and all the wall was joined together unto the half thereof: for the people had a mind to work. But it came to pass, that when **Sanballat, and Tobiah, and the Arabians, and the Ammonites, and the Ashdodites, heard that the walls of Jerusalem were made up, and that the breaches began to be stopped, then they were very wroth, And conspired all of them together to come and to fight against Jerusalem, and to hinder it.** Nevertheless we made our prayer unto our God, and set a watch against them day and night, because of them.*
>
> NEHEMIAH 4:6-9

Notice that there was conspiracy to hinder and stop the walls from being rebuilt. The rebuilding of the wall represented the rekindling of hope and life and the enemies of God's people were very angry. You need to understand that when you rebuild the wall of your life, not everybody will be happy for you. The Sanballats and Tobiahs of this world are still here and they will conspire to stop you. You've got to have the same attitude as Nehemiah: '*Nevertheless, we made our prayer...*' In other words, '*irrespective of what you, people or devils do and say, we really don't care; we are moving forward and will keep on praying.*' So a strong spirit will resist the thwarting of destiny. A strong spirit will resist any plot of conspiracy. You resist an attempt made against your destiny because God in His Word has declared, '*To subvert a man in his cause, the Lord approveth not.*' (Lamentations 3:36). Therefore anyone and anything trying to stop, thwart or stonewall your destiny has been disapproved by God.

﹩ Resist witchcraft

A strong spirit will not turn and cower before witchcraft but will resist it. I remember, as a young minister, Bishop Cyril Demba gave me this advice: '*Glenn, you will not understand it now but later you will. Your greatest fight in ministry will be witchcraft. You need to learn to fight, resist and overcome witchcraft.*' I must admit as a young man I did not understand but the older I become the more I understand. As a young minister, I did not grasp what he was saying about witchcraft because of pre-conceived ideas. When one thinks of witchcraft, one tends to think about people with feathers in their head, a skull necklace around their neck, cutting a chicken and shedding its blood. This is one level of witchcraft and of course we have authority over it in the name of Jesus. This level of witchcraft is visible and in the open. There is a more subtle aspect of witchcraft that we do not pay attention to. One of the meanings of witchcraft is 'that which is hidden' and because it is hidden many are oblivious to it.

*Now as Jannes and Jambres **withstood Moses,** so do these also resist the truth: men of corrupt minds, reprobate concerning the faith.*

2 TIMOTHY 3:8

Jannes and Jambres were the two chief sorcerers and wizards of Pharaoh. Their whole purpose was to stop the Word that God gave to Moses and to stop his ministry from being fulfilled. Paul also had the same issue:

*And when they had gone through the isle unto Paphos, they found a **certain sorcerer,** a false prophet, a Jew, whose name was Bar-jesus: Which was with the deputy of the country, Sergius Paulus, a prudent man; who called for Barnabas and Saul, and desired to hear the word* *of God. But Elymas the sorcerer (for so is his name by interpretation) withstood them, seeking to turn away the deputy from the faith."*

ACTS 13:6-8

Philip and Peter also had to deal with witchcraft. Philip dealt with Simon and then Peter had to deal with him:

*But there was a certain man, called **Simon, which beforetime in the same city used sorcery, and bewitched the people of Samaria,** giving out that himself was some great one: **To whom they all gave heed, from the least to the greatest,** saying, This man is the great power of God. And to him they had regard, because that **of long time he had bewitched them with sorceries.***

ACTS 8:9-11

To be bewitched means that a spell has been cast over and on someone putting the latter in a trance so that he cannot resist but does the will of another and does things that they would not normally do. It also means to be *under* a spell. Simon had the whole of Samaria under his spell. Elymas sought to put Sergius Paulus under his spell to resist the preaching of Paul. Witchcraft seeks to oppose the Word of God. It seeks to turn people away from the truth. Paul said to the Galatian believers, '*O foolish Galatians, who hath bewitched you, that ye should not obey the truth*' (Galatians 3:1). Witchcraft is when people hear the Word of God, know it to be the truth and still will not obey it. Many pastors are frustrated due to the fact that even though they are preaching and teaching their hearts out, they are not seeing the changes in the people's lives like they desire and for some unknown reason their ministry is not flourishing. There is always opposition and obstruction. Many are preaching and no one is getting saved. There are churches and ministers who have not seen a sinner converted for years. This is the spirit of witchcraft opposing the church and minister. Like Paul and Moses who were strong in their spirit they broke through the resistance and went into their destiny. So will you!

> *Witchcraft is when people hear the Word of God,*
> *know it to be the truth and still will not obey it*

♂ Resist sin and sicknesses

A person with a strong spirit is not a carnal believer who easily succumbs and yields to sin. Nor does a person with a strong spirit easily yield or surrender to the spirit of infirmities. You have to look at sickness the same way you look at sin: both are to be resisted.

> *Let not sin therefore reign in your mortal body, that ye should obey it in the lusts thereof. Neither yield ye your members as instruments of unrighteousness unto sin: but yield yourselves unto God, as those that are alive from the dead, and your members as instruments of righteousness unto God. For sin shall not have dominion over you: for ye are not under the law, but under grace. What then? shall we sin, because we are not under the law, but under grace? God forbid. Know ye not, that to whom ye yield yourselves servants to obey, his servants ye are to whom ye obey; whether of sin unto death, or of obedience unto righteousness?*
> ROMANS 6:12-16

A blood-bought and blood-washed believer, whose anchor is in the Cross and the Word will be strong enough spiritually to resist temptation. Jesus told the disciples, '*The spirit is willing but the flesh is weak*' and this is why they fell into temptation. A weak spirit will yield to the lust of the flesh very easily. It will yield its member to the fruit of unrighteousness whereas a strong spirit person will yield his body unto righteousness. Like Joseph, '*Flee also youthful lusts: but follow righteousness, faith, charity, peace, with them that call on the Lord out of a pure heart.*' (2 Timothy 2:22). Sometimes the best form of resisting sin is to run.

A strong spirit will resist and stand tall when attacked by the spirit of infirmities. This is why the Amplified Bible rendition of this verse is valuable: *The strong spirit of a man sustains him in bodily pain or trouble...*' A strong spirit resists sickness knowing that our redemption in Christ has made provision for both the sin and sickness problem.

THE VIRTUES OF A STRONG SPIRIT 1-4

A strong spirit will resist and stand tall when
attacked by the spirit of infirmities

Virtue 4

A strong spirit does not look to the natural for hope but derives its hope supernaturally from God's promises

Abraham was a man of strong faith and strong spirit. Paul disclosed the secret of Abraham in the epistle to the Romans:

> *Who against hope believed in hope, that he might become the father of many nations; according to that which was spoken, So shall thy seed be. And being not weak in faith, he considered not his own body now dead, when he was about an hundred years old, neither yet the deadness of Sara's womb.*
>
> ROMANS 4:18-19

Abraham's hope did not come from his body. Paul unveiled to us that by the time Abraham was ninety-nine, his body was impotent and his wife's body clock had stopped working a long time ago. In the natural, this looked like an impossible situation; completely hopeless. However Abraham's hope did not come from the physical as there was nothing in the natural to give him a shred of hope. As far as his and her body clocks were concerned, they were kaput. As far as medical science was concerned, this was beyond anything the best and brightest doctors could ever fix. As far as nature was concerned, that boat had sailed out a long time ago and they missed it. But in the midst of all this hopelessness and negativity, God had already spoken a word of promise. Abraham had supernatural hope from the voice of God's promise.

A believer whose spirit is strong will derive his joy from what God has said irrespective of what the world, the flesh and the devil are saying. You will possess the same kind of attitude that Paul had when he was thrown into jail for preaching the Gospel with the view of no release.

Supernatural hope comes from the voice of God's promise

---

*For I know that this shall **turn to my salvation** through your prayer, and the supply of the Spirit of Jesus Christ, **According to my earnest expectation and my hope, that in nothing I shall be ashamed,** but that with all boldness, as always, so now also Christ shall be magnified in my body, whether it be by life, or by death.*

PHILIPPIANS 1:19-20

Although the authorities had planned to keep him locked up, Paul had supernatural hope and expectation that the situation would turn for his betterment. That's a man with a strong spirit!

CHAPTER 5
THE VIRTUES OF A STRONG SPIRIT 5-8

W E are continuing to look at the virtues of a strong spirit and how it benefits us tremendously by repealing and rejecting the attacks of the devil.

Virtue 5

A strong spirit enables you to receive from God while a weak spirit makes you subject to receive from the devil

The stronger your spirit is the more and the quicker you can receive from God. The weaker your spirit is the more and the quicker you can receive from the devil. In life you will meet people who easily receive from God: it seems whatever they believe for and pray for, they receive. They are quick to be healed; they are quick to receive breakthroughs and many victories. Yes, they go through trials and testings but they turn their testings into testimonies. For other believers everything that can go wrong will go wrong. They are always sick. Whenever the Flu season comes, they are the first to get it. Things go from bad to worse. Why? It is all dependent upon the conditioning of their spirit man. A strong spirit acts like a magnet, pulling on the things of God and a weak spirit acts like a magnet towards fear, failure and calamity. God has a plan for your life, containing many good things. On the other hand, Satan also has a plan for your life, containing many bad things.

A strong spirit acts like a magnet pulling on the things of God and a weak spirit acts like a magnet towards fear, failures and calamities

---

God has victory for you	Satan has defeat for you
God has divine health for you	Satan has sickness and disease for you
God has abundant life for you	Satan has death for you
God has prosperity for you	Satan has poverty for you
God has peace of mind for you	Satan has fear and worry for you
God has pleasure for you	Satan has pain for you
God has blessings for you	Satan has curses for you
God has joy in the Holy Ghost for you	Satan has depression and stress for you

The question to ask yourself is this, 'From whose hand do I want to receive?' Do you want to receive from God or do you want to receive from Satan? This is why the condition and the shape of your spirit matters. I certainly do not want to be subject to receive from Satan; I want to receive from God. There can be nothing good that comes from the devil. Being weak predisposes you to receive from the handouts of the enemy whereas being strong in spirit positions you to receive from the Almighty.

We see this reality play out every year in the natural. Every year when the season changes and winter approaches, you will see commercials on television and outdoor signs from your local Walgreens, 'Flu season is here. Come and get your flu shot.' I am sure you have seen the commercials and the signs. They are especially geared towards the elderly and young children. However the emphasis is upon the elderly. Why? Because nature has taught us that the elderly are more susceptible to the flu because their immune system is weaker compared to the younger adult. What would not necessarily bother a young adult would bother an elderly person.

Just like a weak immune system makes you vulnerable to receive diseases, a weak spirit makes you vulnerable to receive from Satan

---

I am certain that you have seen, on a Friday and Saturday night in the middle of a freezing winter, young people going to have fun with their friends and are barely wearing anything but a t-shirt and jeans and the young ladies just a dress and high heels. You, on the other hand, are wearing all kinds of layers of clothing just to keep warm yet they seem oblivious to the weather. An elderly person would not do that because it would have a direct effect upon their health. It all comes down to how strong or weak your immune system is. Just like a weak immune system makes you vulnerable to receive diseases, a weak spirit makes you vulnerable to receive from Satan.

As far I am concerned, and I am sure the same is true for you, I want to receive from God everything that belongs to me through my redemption. These blessings, even though they belong to us, are not automatic: faith is the prerequisite to make them living realities in our lives. Therefore take the time to develop and maximize your spirit man.

Virtue 6

A strong spirit enables you to maintain what you have obtained from God.

This is very important for you to grasp as it is one thing to obtain a miracle or blessing but it is a different ball game altogether to be able to keep and maintain it. I do not know how many times I have seen this heartbreaking reality in the lives of so many of God's people who have a temporary breakthrough only to lead to a permanent setback. Let me give you an all too common example. How many times have you seen people standing up in church and testifying how the Lord has healed them of a disease. Everybody clapped and rejoiced with them only for a year later to be attending their funeral. Sometimes people scratched their heads and asked, 'Did God really heal them in the first place.' Yes, he surely did but it is just that the healing was not tenable on their part. The same scenario has taken place with people who obtained a house, a car and promotion but later on, lost them. It simply demonstrates that they could not maintain what they obtained. When the enemy re-attacked and applied the pressure it became too heavy to maintain. It does not mean that they were bad people or faithless people, only that they were not strong enough to maintain what they originally obtained.

♫ River Monsters Example

I travel extensively and tend not to watch television when I'm on the road. This is where I take the time to write a lot of my books. However when I am home I do like to watch some T.V. programs. I like the Sports Channel and watch a lot of English Premier League games. I also like to watch comedies but one of the greatest things I like to watch is fishing programs and one in particular, called River Monsters. It is a British and American wildlife documentary produced for Animal Planet where a man named Jeremy Wade goes all around the world to catch unusual and fearsome killers or predators. It is a fascinating program. I love it! I was amazed to find that there is no one-size-fits-all rod to catch all fish. There have been times when the fish was on the hook but because the line was not strong enough for the pulling force and power of the fish, the line broke. Sometimes it needs to be a custom designed rod. In one of the episodes the idea was to catch the biggest and fastest fish in the world. He set out to catch a sailfish and in order for him to catch this bad boy he had to have a custom-designed fishing rod. This was not like catching a tilapia or a blue gill, this was going to be the biggest and fastest fish in the world. To come up with the ideal fishing pole, he had one built with components from three different countries. I was fascinated to hear this fact. He did not just pick up any old rod and go his merry way to catch that fish. If my memory serves me right, the rod was custom made in America, the reeling mechanism or spinning reel was from Japan and the line and hook were from Germany. It had to be strong in order to bring the fish in. Other, regular poles would serve just as well to hook this fish but would not be able to bring the catch in as either the line or other component of the pole would break. We have seen it time and time again when someone gets all excited for a fish to bite on their hook, but when they try to bring it in the line or rod breaks. This makes it is even worse when you realize how close it was.

Once I was watching a blue marlin fishing competition on the television and when that fish finally bit onto the bait, the battle was on to bring that marlin home to the boat. But the fisherman could not just hook this fish out. In fact he had to sit down in a chair and fasten a seatbelt around him. Why? So that the fish would not pull him out of the boat. Most of these marlin are bigger and heavier than the people fishing for them and it takes time to bring these fish in as they would fight all the way. See this example below of a crew of fishermen catching an 848 pound marlin. This was published in June 2015 by KHON, a Fox Affiliated station in Hawaii:

> *Fishermen always talk about the big one that got away. This time, it's all about the one they reeled in, a marlin weighing nearly half a ton. KHON wanted to know what it takes to bring in such a huge catch.*
>
> *The massive fish towered about twice the height of the crew that reeled it in, an 848-pound marlin that put up quite a fight. The crew of the boat Corcoran tells KHON it took nearly 16 hours to finally land the fish, and it was fighting the whole way.*
>
> *"Reeling until my arm just locked up completely I couldn't do anything about it they had to massage me they were dumping water on me feeding me Gatorade it was very intense," said fisherman Chuck O'Neill. "It's probably the hardest thing I've ever done in my life and my body is beaten right now."*
>
> *The crew tells us they saw the marlin jumping in and out of the water from afar, and thought maybe it was a pretty good sized fish, about 400 pounds.*
>
> *Little did they know it would be more than twice that size, and that it would give them the fight of their lives.*

*"We had the fish up close to the boat over a hundred times and it screamed the reel and took as much line as it could every time," said fisherman Mike Von Wigandt. "And that's where the expertise of these guys, the captain backing down nonstop chasing the fish. **We hooked up near Ko Olina and we ended up bringing the fish to the boat at Kaena Point about two miles offshore so we traveled about 23 miles backwards in circles all night long,"** said Von Wigandt.*

The men were participating in the first annual Kewalo Harbor Big Fish Chase, put together by Ward Village and Howard Hughes Corporation.

The crew won the competition for bringing in the biggest marlin along with a $4,000 prize.

Organizers tell us it's still not close to the world record for the largest marlin caught with a rod and reel, which weighed in at 1,805 pounds. But they'll enjoy this one with friends and their family for a long time.

"This is an amazing experience I will not soon forget that's for sure so I feel very fortunate," said O'Neill.

Manolo Morales
Published: June 8, 2015

Please note it was a big fight to bring that marlin in. It came close to the boat over 100 times but still they could not get it in the boat. That fish was fighting back and did not want to get in the boat. It would swim to the left then swing to the right. **Fighting for 16 hours. Sometimes it felt like it was getting away as it took all the line that it could.** Can you imagine? Look at what the man said, "Reeling until my arm just locked up completely I couldn't do anything about it, they had to massage me, they were dumping water on me feeding me Gatorade, it was very intense." Wow! If only believers had the same resolve. The marlin gave them the fight of their lives but they also gave the marlin the fight of its life. As long as that marlin was still on the hook, it was just a matter of time before it was going to be in the boat, *as long as* the fishing crew did not give up. After 16 hours and many miles they caught the biggest fish they had ever caught. The battle was intense and it seemed like it was taking forever but after all was said and done the victory was sweet. They maintained what they obtained with a fight. Paul admonished us:

> **Fight the good fight of faith**, *lay hold on eternal life, whereunto thou art also called, and hast **professed a good profession** before many witnesses. I give thee charge in the sight of God, who quickeneth all things, and before Christ Jesus, who before Pontius Pilate **witnessed a good confession**.*
>   1 TIMOTHY 6:12-13

> *Let us hold fast the profession of our faith without wavering; (for he is faithful that promised;)*
>   HEBREWS 10:23

After 16 hours of fighting, reeling and sometimes feeling like it was getting away with all the line it could, the marlin was brought home and they received a prize

---

We need to fight to maintain what we have obtained from God. You see in order to bring in that big marlin, the rod had to be strong and stand the pressure. The spinning reel had to be able to endure the pull of an 848 pound fish. The line and hook had to remain unbreakable under the fighting skills of the fish. *Strength, tenacity* and *endurance* brought this big marlin home as a prize. You see the miracle the you are believing God for is not a blue gill size miracle but a blue marlin miracle. It is going to take the fight of faith, which is the fight of confession and patience, to bring your miracle home in your boat. As long as that fish is on your hook and you have resolved to '...*stand in the evil day, having done all to stand, stand therefore...*' (Ephesians 6:13, 14), it is just a matter of time before you receive the prize.

Just as all the components of the pole had to be strong, all components of your life – your spirit, soul (mind, will and emotions) and body – have to be strong, to outlast your enemy and win the fight of life.

Virtue 7

A strong spirit always rejoices. It has the spirit of praise with joy in the Holy Ghost and the spirit of faith in Him.

*He staggered not at the promise of God through unbelief; but was **strong in faith**, giving glory to God.*

ROMANS 4:20

Rejoice in the Lord alway: and again I say, Rejoice.

PHILIPPIANS 4:4

Strong faith gives strong praise to God. Many years ago, Smith Wigglesworth said, "Any man can be changed by faith, no matter how he may be fettered." It does not matter what you are going through right now, strong faith and strong praise will take you out to the winning side. Mr Wigglesworth also said, "Faith laughs at impossibilities." How true this is! This great apostle of faith also said, "All the impossibility is with us when we measure God by the limitations of our unbelief." A believer with a strong spirit will have a praise in his heart and mouth. The spirit of faith is the spirit of praise and the spirit of joy in action. Joy in the Holy Ghost will defeat the devil every time. Joy in the Holy Ghost will confuse demon spirits and cause a divine shift in the realm of the spirit on your behalf. Notice that it says Abraham was strong in faith by giving glory to God. Abraham broke decades of fruitlessness by praising the Almighty in the midst of impotence, old age and barrenness. See what the apostle Paul said to the Roman saints:

*For the kingdom of God is not meat and drink; but righteousness, and peace, and **joy in the Holy Ghost**.*

ROMANS 14:17

Joy in the Holy Ghost is the antidote to depression, unforgiveness, bitterness, the spirit of heaviness and constant whining which are abortive forces to your miracles. An antidote is something that counteracts or neutralizes an unpleasant feeling or situation. When barrenness and failure were boldly staring Abraham in the face, he counteracted and neutralized them by giving God unrestrained praise. As a matter of fact, the same thing happen to Sarah in order for her to receive strength to conceive what God had promised. Paul explains this to the Galatians:

> For it is written, that Abraham had two sons, **the one by a bondmaid, the other by a freewoman.** But he who was of the bondwoman was born after the flesh; **but he of the freewoman was by promise.** Which things are an allegory: for these are the two covenants; the one from the mount Sinai, which gendereth to bondage, which is Agar. **For this Agar is mount Sinai in Arabia, and answereth to Jerusalem which now is, and is in bondage with her children. But Jerusalem which is above is free,** which is the mother of us all. For it is written, **Rejoice, thou barren that bearest not; break forth and cry,** thou that travailest not: for the desolate hath many more children than she which hath an husband.
>
> GALATIANS 4:22-27

Joy in the Holy Ghost is the antidote to depression, unforgiveness, bitterness, spirit of heaviness, constant whining which are abortive forces to your miracles

Paul goes on to explain that Abraham had two sons by two different women, Hagar and Sarah. Hagar was the bondwoman, (Mount Sinai which genders bondage) and Sarah was the freewoman (Jerusalem from above and the mother of us all). How did Sarah break nine decades of fruitlessness? Simply by rejoicing! *'Rejoice O Barren! Sing, O Barren!'* (Isaiah 54:1). Sarah began to rejoice and she gave birth to 'Isaac', which means *laughter*. You see laughter broke decades of barrenness. A strong spirited believer will laugh at the devil, rejoicing, shouting, dancing and singing praise unto the Lord. Both Abraham and Sarah laughed and praised their way out of barrenness and into fruitfulness. They laughed and praised their way out of failure and into fulfillment.

Joy in the Holy Ghost will defeat the devil every time

---

§ **Why laughter?**

Sometimes we want to complicate matters and do hard things to get our miracles but God has chosen the foolish things of this world to confound the wise. God simply says, 'Laugh and rejoice.' Now look at what the Scripture says in Job:

> At destruction and famine thou shalt laugh: neither shalt thou be afraid of the beasts of the earth.
>
> JOB 5:22

That sounds like what Smith Wigglesworth said, "Faith laughs at impossibilities." God said it first! Why would God tell you to do this? Doesn't He know what you are going through? Yes He does! God is not telling you to do something that He Himself has not done:

> Why do the heathen rage, and the people imagine a vain thing? The kings of the earth set themselves, and the rulers take counsel together, against the Lord, and against his anointed, saying, Let us break their bands asunder, and cast away their cords from us. He that sitteth in the heavens shall laugh: the Lord shall have them in derision.
>
> PSALM 2:1-4

The heathens are raging and plotting against God. The kings of the earth and the rulers have plotted a conspiracy to remove God from society. This is pretty much what we are seeing today from ungodly liberal leaders in government. What did God do?

'He that sitteth in the heavens laugh.'

He did not panic! God who is seated in the heavens laughed. He knows that He is God and that He is the Creator. He does not have a need for men to validate Him. He was God before man came along and He will be God after man is dead and buried in the grave. There was a time when, due to Israel's sin, the Philistines captured the ark of God. The people wept and Phinehas' wife died while she was giving birth and called her son, 'Ichabod' meaning *the glory has departed from Israel*. The Philistines gloatingly took the ark and put it in the temple of Dagon, their god as a trophy. Israel may have lost the glory but God still had His glory. In the morning when they rose up and went into the temple, Dagon had fallen on his face before the ark of the covenant. The people picked up Dagon and once again reinstated him in his place but when they came back the next day, Dagon was on the floor again with his head removed and his hands cut off. This simply means whatever conspiracy was in the head of Dagon failed before the Lord and whatever the hands of Dagon were plotting to do came to a stop as they were cut off. You see God is God all by Himself. He knows who He is and He stays seated when His enemies plot against Him.

ᔕ How does that apply to you?

God laughs at His enemies and He tells you to laugh at your famine and destruction. In other words He is telling you to act exactly like Him because you are in Him:

Be ye therefore followers of God, as dear children

EPHESIANS 5:1

Followers simply means *imitators*. We are to imitate God as we are Christ's. Paul reveals our present position in Christ to the Ephesians:

But God, who is rich in mercy, for his great love wherewith he loved us,
Even when we were dead in sins, hath quickened us together with Christ,

(by grace ye are saved;) **And hath raised us up together, and made us sit together in heavenly places in Christ Jesus**

EPHESIANS 2:4-6

Your present position is in heavenly places in Christ seated together with Him. If God, who sits in the heavenly places, can laugh at His enemies, so can you as you are also sitting in these heavenly places.

Having joy in the Holy Ghost means being drunk on the wine of the Spirit and it involves praising, shouting, dancing and laughing. Tapping into this phenomenon triggers the rivers of glory in your life.

❖ When glory manifests, grief is replaced;
❖ When glory manifests, burdens are lifted;
❖ When glory manifests, yokes are destroyed.

Peter, in his first epistle, was encouraging the believers who were scattered because of great trials. He said:

Whom having not seen, ye love; in whom, though now ye see him not, yet believing, ye rejoice with joy unspeakable and full of glory: Receiving the end of your faith, even the salvation of your souls.

1 PETER 1:8-9

Allow me to paraphrase what Peter penned: 'You don't see him presently but you still believe and in the middle of your believing you are rejoicing with joy unspeakable, releasing the glory to enable you to receive the end of your faith.' You see, between believing and receiving there has to be joy. Jesus told us in Mark's Gospel, *'Therefore I say unto you, What things soever ye desire, when ye pray, believe that ye receive them, and ye shall have them.'* (Mark 11:24). Then Peter shed some more light on it, informing us that we must rejoice in the middle of our believing to receive like Abraham. A believer with a strong spirit is like Paul when he wrote to the Philippians from prison. He was thrown in jail for preaching the Gospel.

Some of his friends were preaching the Gospel because they knew he was set for the defense of the Gospel but his enemies were preaching out of spite just to add more to his affliction. In other words they wanted to pile on the misery for Paul. What was Paul's attitude:

> *What then? notwithstanding, every way, whether in pretence, or in truth, Christ is preached; and **I therein do rejoice, yea, and will rejoice.** For I know that this shall turn to my salvation through your prayer, and the supply of the Spirit of Jesus Christ*
>
> PHILIPPIANS 1:18-19

I really like the way the Message translation renders this passage in Philippians: '*I want to report to you, friends, that my imprisonment here has had the opposite of its intended effect. Instead of being squelched, the Message has actually prospered... So how am I to respond? **I've decided that I really don't care** about their motives, whether mixed, bad, or indifferent. Every time one of them opens his mouth, Christ is proclaimed, so **I just cheer them on! And I'm going to keep that celebration going because I know how it's going to turn out...**'* (Philippians 1:12, 18-19 – Message Translation).

❖ You ought to tell the devil, 'I've decided I really don't care what you do, I am going to rejoice, yes, I will rejoice and keep that celebration going because I know how this is going to turn out. It's going to be breakthroughs all the way.'

❖ You ought to look at your piles of bills and debt and say, 'I've decided I really don't care what you do, I'm going to keep my celebration going until I am debt free.'

❖ You ought to look at the devil and tell him, 'I've decided I really don't care what you do, I'm going to keep my celebration going until my victory manifests.'

❖ You ought to tell that sickness afflicting you right now, 'I've decided I really don't care what you do, I'm going to keep my celebration going until my healing paid for by Jesus manifests.'

The same thing that happened to Paul will happen to you. Whatever the devil motioned against you will have the opposite intended effect. Paul praised and danced his way out of jail. He did the same thing when he was in jail with Silas. There is an old saying in the world that goes like this: 'I'm laughing all the way to the bank.' Well, you are going to laugh all the way to your prosperity. You will laugh all the way to your breakthrough. You will laugh all the way to your healing and divine health. That's Scriptural!

A merry heart doeth good like a medicine: but a broken spirit drieth the bones.

PROVERBS 17:22

Praise, shout, dance and laugh all the way to your victory

Let Habakkuk tell you how to act when life is not working out well for you:

*Although the fig tree shall not blossom, neither shall fruit be in the vines; the labour of the olive shall fail, and the fields shall yield no meat; the flock shall be cut off from the fold, and there shall be no herd in the stalls: **Yet I will rejoice in the Lord, I will joy in the God of my salvation.** The Lord God is my strength, and he will make my feet like hinds' feet, and he will make me to walk upon mine high places. To the chief singer on my stringed instruments.*

HABAKKUK 3:17-19

When you read these verses, they are enough to get you into a severe depression. By all accounts Habakkuk should have been going out of his mind. Nothing was working! Someone in the world would say, 'No fruit, no meat, no flock, no harvest, no herd and no luck.' But Habakkuk said, 'Yet I will rejoice, I will joy in the God of my salvation.' That's a man with a strong spirit, rejoicing and praising in the midst of lack! What was the end result:

❖ The Lord God is my strength, and he will make my feet like hinds' feet. He will accelerate my destiny.

❖ He will make me to walk upon mine high places. I will still be promoted.

---

*Habakkuk teaches you that your praise is
your pathway to your promotion*

Nehemiah told us, '*The joy of the Lord is our strength.*' (Nehemiah 8:10). The more you have joy in your God, the stronger your spirit will be. I really love the way the Message Bible renders the verses in Habakkuk:

"*Though the **cherry trees don't blossom and the strawberries don't ripen,** Though the **apples are worm-eaten and the wheat fields stunted,** Though the **sheep pens are sleepless and the cattle barns empty,** I'm singing joyful praise to God. I'm turning cartwheels of joy to my Savior God. Counting on God's Rule to prevail, I take heart and gain strength. I run like a deer. I feel like I'm king of the mountain!*"

HABAKKUK 3:17-19 – MESSAGE TRANSLATION

I love it! I'm going to merge the verses in Habakkuk and Paul's words to the Philippians together from the Message Translation to reveal what our mode of operation should be: '*I'm singing joyful praise to God. I'm turning cartwheels of joy to my Savior God. I feel like I'm king of the mountain... my problem here has had the opposite of its intended effect... I've decided that I really don't care... I'm going to keep that celebration going because I know how it's going to turn out... God's Rule will prevail, I take heart and gain strength. I run like a deer.*'

---

*A believer with a strong spirit rejoices
knowing that God's rule will prevail*

Virtue 8

A strong spirit makes things look easy which are hard for others

Have you ever met people for whom everything seems like hard work. Life is so difficult and they don't mind letting you know that life is not fair. Yet you look at others who are going through tougher times than them but seem like they are breezing through life. What's the difference? The condition of their spirit.

> *If you faint in the day of adversity, your strength is small.*
> PROVERBS 24:10 – AMPLIFIED BIBLE

The strength he is referring to is strength in the spirit. In fact Paul prayed for the Ephesians, when he was going through a lot of tribulations:

> *Wherefore **I desire that ye faint not at my tribulations for you,** which is your glory. For this cause I bow my knees unto the Father of our Lord Jesus Christ, Of whom the whole family in heaven and earth is named, **That he would grant you, according to the riches of his glory, to be strengthened with might by his Spirit in the inner man.***
> EPHESIANS 3:13-16

Apparently the Ephesians were all shaken up about the testings that Paul was going through. However Paul was not the one fainting. His trials bothered them more than they bothered him. So he prayed for them not to faint but to be strengthened with might in the inner man. That's where real strength is! Solomon said that if you faint in the day of adversity then your strength is small. This would indicate a weak spirit. If anyone had a strong spirit, it was Paul. This is the same man who said:

> *For which cause **we faint not;** but though our outward man perish, yet the inward man is renewed day by day. **For our light affliction, which is but for a moment, worketh for us a far more** exceeding and eternal weight of glory.*
> 2 CORINTHIANS 4:16-17

Paul said:

* ❖ We faint not – I am not gong down;
* ❖ Our light affliction – my problems are light;
* ❖ Work for us far more – my problems are working for me.

Only a man with a strong spirit can say, 'My problems are light and they are working for me.' Many others in his place would be falling apart. Do you remember when Agabus prophesied on Paul about his journey to Jerusalem?

> *And as we tarried there many days, there came down from Judæa a certain prophet, named Agabus. And when he was come unto us, he took Paul's girdle, and bound his own hands and feet, and said, Thus saith the Holy Ghost,* **So shall the Jews at Jerusalem bind the man that owneth this girdle, and shall deliver him into the hands of the Gentiles. And when we heard these things, both we, and they of that place, besought him not to go up to Jerusalem.**
>
> ACTS 21:10-12

This was not the kind of prophecy that you hear today, 'Yay, saith the Lord – Even as I opened the Red Sea for Moses, I have opened, yay, yay and yay saith the Lord thy God, the Omnipotent thine way, yay verily thy way is opened before thee. Now go forth – yay'

Only a man with a strong spirit can say, 'My problems are light and they are working for me.'

This was not the kind of prophetic word that gave goosebumps. Remember that Agabus had a track record as a prophet of God. He prophesied about a famine which came to pass in the days of Claudius Ceasar (Acts 11:28). So this was not a lightweight prophet but a heavy hitter and well respected. What was the reaction?

And when we heard these things, both we, and they of that place, besought him not to go up to Jerusalem.

ACTS 21:12

Apparently Philip's daughters, wife and Luke had a commotion of tears and fears after they heard this prophecy. In other words, 'Paul! Agabus doesn't miss it, he's very accurate in prophecies, and you're as good as dead.' What was Paul's reaction:

Then Paul answered, What mean ye to weep and to break mine heart? for I am ready not to be bound only, but also to die at Jerusalem for the name of the Lord Jesus. And when he would not be persuaded, we ceased, saying, The will of the Lord be done. And after those days we took up our carriages, and went up to Jerusalem.

ACTS 21:13-15

Paul was already aware of the situation in his spirit and he would not be dissuaded. Only a man with a strong spirit can speak like this. Where others were cowering, he was boasting in the Lord. A strong spirit makes things look easy which are hard for others. Allow me to remind you of the posture of Jesus when he was in the storm, with his disciples in the same boat:

*And there arose a great storm of wind, and the waves beat into the ship, so that it was now full. **And he was in the hinder part of the ship, asleep on a pillow:** and they awake him, and say unto him, **Master, carest thou not that we perish?***

MARK 4:37-38

You see the disciples had death on their minds even with the Master in their ship. Jesus on the other hand was sleeping in the hinder part of the ship on a pillow. While the storm was hard for the disciples, Jesus made it look easy. Being strong in spirit is not automatic simply because you are born again. Now look at this great example. We know that Dr. Luke wrote his second treatise to Theophilus, which we call the book of Acts today. He was also a traveling companion with Paul and this is why he had first-hand accounts of the missionary journeys and experiences of Paul. In Acts 27, Luke was accompanying Paul – who was arrested – and was set to go to Italy to appear before Ceasar. Paul had warned the centurion, due to the perception which he had in his spirit, that trouble was ahead. The latter preferred to listen to the professional master of the ship and since it looked like the weather was fine, overruled Paul's warning. However Paul was proven to be right as they ran into a storm called a Euroclydon. They were caught unawares and that storm battered the ship. Then they got stuck in quicksands. They also threw all their goods off the ship. They were in dire straits and Dr Luke penned those words:

And when neither sun nor stars in many days appeared, and no small tempest lay on us, all hope that we should be saved was then taken away.

ACTS 27:20

§ Two believers in the same boat

Luke hadn't seen the sun or stars for fourteen days and his conclusion was, 'All hope that we should be saved was taken away.' Paul on the other hand, was in a different frame of mind:

But after long abstinence Paul stood forth in the midst of them, and said, Sirs, ye should have hearkened unto me, and not have loosed from Crete, and to have gained this harm and loss. And now I exhort you to **be of good cheer: for there shall be no loss of any man's life among you,** *but of the ship.* **For there stood by me this night the angel of God, whose I am, and whom I serve,** *Saying, Fear not, Paul; thou must be brought before Cæsar: and, lo, God hath given thee all them that sail with thee.* **Wherefore, sirs, be of good cheer: for I believe God, that it shall be even as it was told me.**

ACTS 27:21-25

Two believers were in the same boat but not in the same mindset; Luke had death on his mind but Paul had life on his mind; Luke was seeing the angel of death approaching but Paul was conversing with the angel of God; Luke was believing in the storm and Paul was believing in God. What was hard for Luke was easy for Paul. A believer with a strong spirit makes things look easy which are hard others. Paul was eating bread and compelled them to eat bread. They didn't feel like eating bread. Paul told them to cheer up. You can hear them say to Paul, 'How can you eat in a moment like this?' They felt like throwing up. Eventually they came to accept Paul's view and cheered up and ate. What was the end result? They were all saved!

---

*Two believers can be in the same boat
but not in the same mindset*

◌ My son Ethan

I travel extensively and we are always shipping books to different nations but I also take books with me on my travels too. We have crates of boxes of books in our ministry but I also keep boxes of books in a specific room in my basement because sometimes it's just easier to take a few boxes and go. One time as I was on my way to Nigeria for a major convention, we had run out of stock of books there so I decided I would not go to the ministry base to get books but take some from my basement. I went down in the basement and started picking some of these boxes and they were heavy. I was sweating. I was griping and fussing carrying one box at a time.

I told my wife, 'You know I don't do any of this in Nigeria and anywhere else. I am treated like a king.'

My wife asked me, 'Are you struggling there?'

Shamefully but gladly I said yes. So she asked my son to help me. My son's name is Ethan and he had just turned 18. That boy has muscles everywhere.

Even his eyebrows have muscles. He works out, has a six pack and eats very healthily. So my wife said to him, 'Can you help your dad with his packing and boxes?' And he went at it, carrying boxes swiftly and even brought up two at a time. My man pride was taking a serious beating and to make it worst, my wife proudly shouted, 'Look at my son!' My inward reaction was, 'Oh yea! Both you and your son can shut up. Just remember you are staying in this house because of my grace and mercy. Unlike God, my mercies might run out this morning!' Then we all laughed. My point is because Ethan is stronger than me he made that which was hard for me look easy. A believer with a strong spirit will make that which is hard for others look like a piece of cake.

CHAPTER 6
THE VIRTUES OF A STRONG SPIRIT 9-12

Virtue 9

A strong spirit acts like a shock absorber or a suspension when you go through life's potholes

If you fall to pieces in a crisis then there was not much to you to begin with.
PROVERBS 24:10 – MESSAGE TRANSLATION

JESUS tells us of the two men who built their houses. One built his house upon the sand and the other built his house upon the strong foundation of the rock. When the storms of life hit both houses at the same time, the one that was built upon the rock stood the test and outlasted the storm. The one built on the sand, as long as there was no storm, looked just as good than the other one. In fact it was quicker to build and erect than the one which was built upon the rock. People would have sung its praises by saying how quick it was built and how it looked just as good as the one built upon the rock. The litmus test came when the storm hit and it could not last. Its ruin was great. This simply means the people living in that house perished with it in the storm (Luke 6:47-49).

The problem with that house was not its decor or ground-up premise but the foundation. When the storm hit, it could not resist the pressure and velocity of the wind. It could not soak up pressure but collapsed under it. One time I was fascinated watching a program on television about earthquakes in Japan and other nations and how some of their skyscrapers are built in such a way as to be flexible and absorb the shock of an earthquake. Some of the buildings even had shock absorbers and wheels at the foundation to reel with the movements rather than being a solid blocks of bricks which crumble when the earth moves from underneath. These wheels act like shock absorbers to temper the earthquake's violent movements. The strong spirit of a believer acts like a shock absorber when life's earthquakes are shaking everything that can be shaken.

I am pretty sure you have been in a car where the suspension was not great and you felt every bump in the road. Yet if you ride In a car with great isuspension, you won't feel the potholes nearly as much. When Paul's life was under a decree of death, he had the answer within him:

> *For we would not, brethren, have you ignorant of **our trouble which came to us** in Asia, that we **were pressed out of measure, above strength, insomuch that we despaired even of life: But we had the sentence of death in ourselves,** that we should not trust in ourselves, but in God which raiseth the dead: Who delivered us from so great a death, and doth deliver: in whom we trust that he will yet deliver us.*
>
> 2 CORINTHIANS 1:8-10

The word 'sentence' here is better translated as 'answer'. When trouble, despair and death came knocking on Paul's door, he had an answer for it. The answer was within his spirit man, trusting in God. He was not shocked to death. The reason people are shocked is because they do not have a shock absorber so everything comes as a shock to them. The reason why they are in suspense and fear is because they do not have a good suspension.

The reason people are shocked and in suspense is because they do not have a shock absorber and good suspension

---

Virtue 10

A strong spirit creates a forcefield around you stopping the intrusion and penetration of the enemy

In the natural, a forcefield is an invisible barrier of exerted strength. It is a barrier made up of energy or particles to protect a person, area or object from attacks or intrusions, or as a means of containment or confinement. You need to do what Solomon said to do, *'Keep your heart with all diligence, for out of it are the issues of life.'* (Proverbs 4: 23). A strong spirit acts like a repellent fending off the works of Satan.

When Jesus was explaining and expounding on the Parable of the sower, he said, *'And the **cares of this world, and the deceitfulness of riches, and the lusts of other things entering in,** choke the word, and it becometh unfruitful.'* (Mark 4:19). Three things that will choke the Word and make your spirit unfruitful are:

❖ Worry
❖ Deceitfulness of riches
❖ Lusts of other things

A believer who is aware of these negative forces will do his utmost to protect his heart from them. These will sap the energy from your spirit. They are drainers designed by the enemy to keep you on his turf. As long as worry, fear, bitterness, anger, doubt, unbelief and double-mindedness have access to your life, you will be a victim of circumstances. This is why it is of major importance for you to build a strong spirit because it acts as a forcefield, stopping negative forces from having a field day in your life.

⸱ Batfink

When I was a kid, growing up in England, I enjoyed watching cartoons. Of course I loved the usual Tom & Jerry, Bugs Bunny, Scooby-Doo, Spider-Man, Superman and Danger Mouse to name a few. But there was one – not my favorite – which caught my attention. It was a cartoon about a superhero bat called Batfink. His super-power was in his wings. When he was attacked or being shot, he would say, 'Your bullets cannot harm me: my wings are like a shield of steel.' When we were kids and my brothers and I were messing around, we would say to each other, 'Your bullets cannot harm me, my wings are a shield of steel.' Well, that's what you should be saying to the devil and the negative forces attacking you. Just tell him, 'Devil, your fears, panic attacks, doubts and darts of worry cannot harm me: my spirit is like a wing of steel.' I've never forgotten that! Remember, *the spirit of a man will sustain his infirmity; but a wounded spirit who can bear?* (Proverbs 18:14).

Virtue 11

A strong spirit enables you to have communion with and be led and guided by the Holy Spirit

Paul made this closing remark to the believers in Corinth: '*The grace of the Lord Jesus Christ, and the love of God, and the communion of the Holy Ghost, be with you all.*' (2 Corinthians 13:14). Communion with the Holy Spirit will promote a strong inner man. The stronger the communion the stronger your spirit will be. The ultimate virtue of having a strong spirit is the enablement of being led by the Spirit. Communion with the Holy Spirit eases and increases your propensity of being led by the Holy Spirit. This is the key to victory in life. We see this reality in the life of Jesus. People have the idea that Jesus, just because He was the Messiah, had everything handed to Him on a plate. That was not the case! The book of Hebrews informed us that, '*Though he were a Son, yet learned he obedience by the things which he suffered.*' (Hebrews 5:8). He did not have things offered to Him on a silver platter; He learned obedience.

Notice what the Gospel of Luke says of the young Jesus:

And the child grew, and waxed strong in spirit, filled with wisdom: and the grace of God was upon him.

LUKE 2:40

He did not just breeze through life saying, 'I'm the Messiah.' No, He waxed strong in spirit. His spirit was strengthened just like yours and mine need to be strengthened. Then Luke also informs us, after Jesus waxed strong in spirit:

*And Jesus being **full of the Holy Ghost returned from Jordan, and was led by the Spirit** into the wilderness*

LUKE 4:1

Look at the sequence: He waxed strong in spirit, was full of the Holy Spirit then was led by the Spirit. This same sequence applies to us too. Apart from Jesus, no one among the writers of the New Testament revealed more of the ministry, character and importance of the Holy Spirit than Paul. Indeed the other disciples were very intimate with the Holy Spirit and were very successful but it was Paul who, as a master craftsman, skillfully unveiled the Spirit of God on a much deeper and personal level to you and I. His success in life and ministry was due to his constant leaning upon the leading of the Spirit of God. After all it was Paul who unveiled:

❖ The nine gifts of the Spirit;
❖ The nine fruit of the Spirit;
❖ The intercessory praying skill of the Spirit;
❖ The consciousness of the indwelling of the Spirit;
❖ The leading of the Spirit;
❖ The inward witness of the Spirit;
❖ The grieving and quenching of the Spirit;
❖ The seal of the Spirit;

- ❖ The supply of the Spirit;
- ❖ The sowing in the Spirit;
- ❖ The constant filling and refilling of the Spirit;
- ❖ The communion of the Spirit.

---

*Communion with the Holy Spirit eases and increases
your propensity of being led by the Holy Spirit*

All the above mentioned, strengthen our spirit man in order to enjoy the leading of the Spirit. In his epistle to the Romans, the eighth chapter, in the space of a few verses, Paul reminds us three times of the abiding and indwelling Sprit:

> *But ye are not in the flesh, but in the Spirit, if so be that **the Spirit of God dwell in you**. Now if any man have not the Spirit of Christ, he is none of his... But **if the Spirit of him that raised up Jesus from the dead dwell in you**, he that raised up Christ from the dead shall also quicken your mortal bodies by his Spirit that dwelleth in you.*
>
> ROMANS 8:9, 11

If, in the space of a couple of verses, Paul is drilling into us the fact that we are indwelt by the Holy Spirit. He was trying to get our attention. What was the purpose of this reminder:

> *Therefore, brethren, we are debtors, not to the flesh, to live after the flesh. For if ye live after the flesh, ye shall die: but if ye through the Spirit do mortify the deeds of the body, ye shall live. For as many as are led by the Spirit of God, they are the sons of God.*
>
> ROMANS 8:12-14

Paul said that we owe nothing to the flesh as the flesh leads us to death. However we are indwelt by the Spirit to be led by the Spirit so that our victory in this life can be secured. The constant communion and consciousness of the indwelling and abiding presence of the Holy Spirit will enable you to walk in and be led by the Spirit. When you are led by the Spirit, you are in good company with Jesus and Paul. A strong spirit will pull and catch the signals of the Spirit when others are oblivious. A strong spirit sharpens your spiritual senses to tap into the things of the Spirit. This is how Paul was aware of a storm when it looked like nothing was brewing over the horizon. This is how Paul knew he needed to go to Macedonia and not Bithynia (Acts 16:6-8).

A strong spirit will pull and catch the signals of
the Spirit while a weak spirit is oblivious to them

Take the time to commune with the Holy Spirit in order to strengthen your spirit man to hear his voice and catch his plans. If you do, you will find rest in your redemption:

Like a herd of cattle led to pasture, the Spirit of God gave them rest.
That's how you led your people!

ISAIAH 63:14

Virtue 12

A strong spirit enables you to minister in the supernatural to your generation.

And Jesus returned in the power of the Spirit into Galilee: and there went out a fame of him through all the region round about.

LUKE 4:14

This is after he waxed strong in spirit and was full and led by the Holy Spirit. He now returns in the power of the Spirit. What was the outcome?

How God anointed Jesus of Nazareth with the Holy Ghost and with power: who went about doing good, and healing all that were oppressed of the devil; for God was with him.

ACTS 10:38

Ye men of Israel, hear these words; Jesus of Nazareth, a man approved of God among you by miracles and wonders and signs, which God did by him in the midst of you, as ye yourselves also know.

ACTS 2:22

The Spirit of the Lord is upon me, because he hath anointed me to preach the gospel to the poor; he hath sent me to heal the brokenhearted, to preach deliverance to the captives, and recovering of sight to the blind, to set at liberty them that are bruised.

LUKE 4:18

The result was a miraculous ministry that met the needs of all humanity. Many would dearly desire to minister supernaturally in their church and ministry, but cannot. Why? Because they are stronger intellectually and theologically than spiritually. As great as theology and intellect can be it will not meet the needs of humanity. If they were so great then many churches would not be empty or turned into apartments. You see, the mainline churches are full of intellectual theologians with no Spirit power. The apostle Paul also testified to this fact: '*...my preaching was not with enticing words of man's wisdom, but in demonstration of the Spirit and of power: That your faith should not stand in the wisdom of men, but in the power of God.*' (1 Corinthians 2:4-5). In addition, he also said this in his closing remarks to the Romans saints:

For I will not dare to speak of any of those things which Christ hath not wrought by me, to make the Gentiles obedient, by word and deed, Through mighty signs and wonders, by the power of the Spirit of God; so that from Jerusalem, and round about unto Illyricum, I have fully preached the gospel of Christ.

ROMANS 15:18-19

You will best serve your generation when you are waxed strong in spirit, are full of the Spirit, are led by the Spirit, tap into the supply of the Spirit and demonstrate the Spirit.

CHAPTER 7
IDENTIFYING THE CONTRASTING TRAITS OF A STRONG AND WEAK SPIRIT

W E have been looking at the virtues of a strong spirit. I have listed twelve dynamic virtues for you. Sometimes the revelation gets stronger and sinks deeper when you look at the flip side of the coin. So in this chapter we want to look at 25 contrasting traits between a strong and a weak spirit. The traits that we expose will indicate whether you are strong in spirit or weak in spirit. You will be able to tell with which you identify more. If you see more traits of weakness then all it indicates is that it is time to give serious consideration to working out the spiritual muscles of you inner man. A man who gave tremendous time to the building of his spirit man was Paul and that is why, when you read his epistles you can sense that even though he went through hardships he remained steady:

We are troubled on every side, yet not distressed; we are perplexed, but not in despair. Persecuted, but not forsaken; cast down, but not destroyed.
                                        2 CORINTHIANS 4:8-9

When you read the words above from Paul, you can tell this man had a strong spirit. Notice these words, 'not distressed, not in despair and not destroyed'. These are the kind of words that reveal an unbeatable spirit of faith lodged deeply within a man. On the other hand, words such as 'troubled every side, distressed, perplexed, forsaken and destroyed' reveal a broken down person. The word *hopeless* should never be associated with a believer:

*Wherefore remember, that ye being in time past Gentiles in the flesh, who are called Uncircumcision by that which is called the Circumcision in the flesh made by hands; **That at that time ye were without Christ,*** *being aliens from the commonwealth of Israel, and strangers from the covenants of promise, having no hope, and without God in the world: But now in Christ Jesus ye who sometimes were far off are made nigh by the blood of Christ.*

EPHESIANS 2:11-13

The only people without hope in the world are those without Christ, without the promise of the Word and without faith. In spite of an impotent body, Abraham still had hope, based upon the spoken promise of God to him (Romans 4:18). Therefore you and I can never say we are hopeless or helpless as we have a covenant with God. To be more exact, we have a better covenant, established upon better promises (Hebrews 8:6). The hallmark of a believer with a strong spirit is that he is *new creation* minded whereas a weak spirit believer is still *old creation* minded despite being a new creation.

---

*The hallmark of a believer with a strong spirit
is that he is new creation minded*

The realities of the new creation play a prominent role in the thought-process and confessions of a strong-spirit believer. He is quick to acknowledge, quick to believe, quick to confess and quick to act upon the Word. He is quicker to believe the report of the Lord than the report of the world. These are certain signposts to let you know whether you have a strong or weak spirit. Let's have a look at 25 contrasting traits between a strong and weak spirit.

1. A strong spirit sustains through anything;
    A weak spirit falls apart.

2. A strong spirit conquers adversity;
    A weak spirit is conquered by adversity and the worries of this world.

3. A strong spirit is cool under pressure;
    A weak spirit loses its decorum under pressure.

4. A strong spirit easily yields to God and his Word;
    A weak spirit constantly argues with the veracity of the Word.

5. A strong spirit has an established and fixed heart trusting in the Lord;
    A weak spirit has a vacillating and troubled heart.

6. A strong spirit praises;
    A weak spirit panics.

7. A strong spirit mentally assents to the truth of the Scriptures and is
    quick to act upon it;
    *A weak spirit mentally assents to the truth of the Scriptures but in
    actions deny its reality.*

8. A strong spirit gives you the power of resistance against the devil and
    temptations;
    A weak spirit succumbs to the devil and temptations.

9. A strong spirit does not look to the natural for hope but derives its
    hope supernaturally from God's promises;
    *A weak spirit is limited to the natural, is quick to be depressed and feels
    hopeless.*

10. A strong spirit enables you to receive from God;
    A weak spirit makes you subject to receive from the devil.

11. A strong spirit enables you to maintain what you have obtained
    from God;
    A weak spirit cannot retain what it obtained from God.

12. A strong spirit always rejoices. It has the spirit of praise with joy in the
    Holy Ghost;
    A weak spirit always gripes, complains and is bitter.

13. A strong spirit makes things look easy which are hard for others, runs through a troop and leaps over walls (Psalm 18:28,29);
A weak spirit makes a mountain out of a molehill, believes all things are hard, gets run over by a troop and finds a wall of obstruction everywhere.

14. A strong spirit overcomes the world, the flesh and the devil;
A weak spirit is easily overwhelmed by the world, the flesh and the devil.

15. A strong spirit never quits even when the battle heats up;
A weak spirit quits the moment the battle heats up.

16. A strong spirit is redemption minded and result minded;
A weak spirit is problem minded and defeat minded.

17. A strong spirit is full of energy and laughter;
A weak spirit is always tired.

18. A strong spirit acts like a shock absorber or suspension when going through life's potholes;
A weak spirit is in shock and suspense.

19. A strong spirit walks by faith and is the expression of the spirit of faith;
A weak spirit walks in fear and is the expression of the spirit of unbelief.

20. A strong spirit creates a forcefield around you, stopping the intrusion and penetration of the enemy;
A weak spirit is penetrated by the cares of this world.

21. A strong spirit is led and guided by the Holy Spirit;
A weak spirit is led by the flesh.

22. A strong spirit is victory minded;
A weak spirit is defeat minded.

23. A strong spirit always looks to, and is easily persuaded by the Word;
    A weak spirit looks to, and is easily persuaded by the world.

24. A strong spirit takes responsibility for their actions;
    A weak spirit blames and is critical of others for their actions.

25. A strong spirit walks in love, repents quickly and keeps no account of wrong done to them;
    A weak spirit walks in strife and bitterness, is slow to repent and keeps account of all wrongs done to then.

CHAPTER 8
TRAINING THE HUMAN SPIRIT – *PART 1*

*Wherefore, my beloved, as ye have always obeyed, not as in my presence only, but now much more in my absence, **work out your own salvation** with fear and trembling.*

PHILIPPIANS 2:12

*For bodily exercise **profiteth little:** but godliness is profitable unto all things, having promise of the life that now is, and of that which is to come.*

1 TIMOTHY 4:8

The strong spirit of a man sustains him in bodily pain or trouble, but a weak and broken spirit who can raise up or bear?

PROVERBS 18:14 AMPC

The apostle Paul was very clear in his intent, '*That he would grant you, according to the riches of his glory, to be strengthened with might by his Spirit in the inner man.*' (Ephesians 3:16). Real strength is in your inner man, in your spirit to be more exact. As great as physical muscles are they cannot sustain you through life's circumstances. This is why Paul said, 'bodily exercise profits a little.' The word 'little' here is best rendered 'season' so in other words, 'bodily exercise profits for a season'. On the other hand, spiritual exercise profits for all seasons. In order for you to be sustained throughout all the seasons of your life it is imperative that you build a very strong inner man. One thing for sure is that is your life will go through many different seasons. As an example David said: '*I have been young and now I am old...*' (Psalm 37:25). There will be many seasons of your life but through them all, it is the conditioning of your sprit that will be the establishment of your life.

Training the human spirit

Now, it becomes utterly important to take the time to build your spirit as you would take the time to build your body. The purpose of training the human spirit is firstly to learn to live from the inside out, working in conjunction with the Holy Spirit, the mind and the physical body, to produce peace and victory in your life. Secondly it is to stretch the capacity of your spirit in order for you to dominate the physical realm. Never forget that when God created man, He created him with words of authority (Genesis 1:26). Since man is a spirit, it was to his inward man that God gave authority. Therefore Adam was to dominate the outside from the inside, rule the exterior from the interior and control the physical from the spiritual. However since Adam fell, mankind has been ruled from the outside in. This is why, for the rest of this chapter, and this is the climax of this book, we want to look at ways to train your human spirit.

The apostle Paul was a great lover of sport and in many of his epistles he used sports as an analogy for spiritual matters. An example a passage containing the references to sports is located in the epistle of Corinthians:

*Know ye not that they which run in a race run all, but one receiveth the prize? So run, that ye may obtain. And **every man that striveth for the mastery is temperate in all things**. Now they do it to obtain a corruptible crown; but we an incorruptible. I therefore so run, not as uncertainly; so fight I, not as one that beateth the air: But I keep under my body, and bring it into subjection: lest that by any means, when I have preached to others, I myself should be a castaway.*

1 CORINTHIANS 9:24-27

Paul also said that he finished his course (2 Timothy 4:7) meaning he had the spiritual stamina and energy to last the distance. Paul had learned the secret to developing a fit and strong spirit. Many are more interested in building a strong physique, and that is good for a season, however you need to give importance to building your spirit. You will not become a spiritual giant just because you have been saved for some time. There are people who have been saved for years but are still spiritually weak and deficient. To be strong spiritually, you must take deliberate actions. We are going to look at the natural and glean spiritual lessons from it. To build a strong physique, you will need to:

1. Change your food and drinking habit;
2. Join a good gym and have a good trainer;
3. Exercise / Workout;
4. Have a partner to motivate;
5. Take supplements;
6. Rest;
7. Be consistent.

We can also apply these seven principles to developing a great spiritual physique.

You will not become a spiritual giant just because you have been saved for some time

---

ৡ Change your food and drinking habits

One of the first things you have to do in order for you to get in shape physically, as well as spiritually, is to watch what you eat and drink. In the natural, you will have to stop junk food and sugary drinks: these are poison to your body. You cannot keep eating garbage and expect to be in great shape. You will be in some kind of shape, just not great shape. In the same way, we have to watch what we are eating and drinking spiritually.

Job said these wonderful words:

...I have esteemed the words of his mouth more than my necessary food.

JOB 23:12

And Jeremiah uttered these words:

Thy words were found, and I did eat them; and thy word was unto me the joy and rejoicing of mine heart: for I am called by thy name, O Lord God of hosts

JEREMIAH 15:16

It is imperative that as you work to reshape your spirit, you pay attention to what you eat. As in the natural we have physical food to feed our bodies so in the spiritual we have the Word of God which is *spirit food* to feed our human spirit. Here are three fundamental ways to feed your human spirit:

Reading and Studying – Your priority must be to know the Word, making it the first and final authority in your life. The reading and studying of the Word is feeding upon spiritual food. Jesus said: '...*The words that I speak unto you, they are spirit and they are life.*' (John 6:63) and the apostle Paul instructed his protégé, Timothy: '*Till I come, give attendance to reading, to exhortation, to doctrine.*' (1 Timothy 4:13) and '*Study to shew thyself approved unto God, a workman that needeth not to be ashamed, rightly dividing the word of truth.*' (2 Timothy 2:15). We know that the Word is our daily manna, just like Israel had their daily manna.

What was the manna? The word 'manna' literally meant, 'What is this?' It was a question posed by the Israelites when they first saw this heavenly nourishment from heaven. Not knowing what it was they simply asked in Hebrew, 'Manna?' meaning 'What is this?' Then Moses went on to give us a description of the manna and its goodness:

And the manna was as coriander seed, and the colour thereof as the colour of bdellium. And the people went about, and gathered it, and ground it in mills, or beat it in a mortar, and baked it in pans, and made cakes of it: and the taste of it was as the taste of fresh oil.

NUMBERS 11:7-8

The manna was a seed. Jesus called the Word 'the seed' in his parable of the sower and Peter labelled it as the *'incorruptible seed which liveth and abideth for ever'* (1 Peter 1:23). What we see in the Old Testament is an example for us in the New Testament. The people went about daily gathering the seed, beat it in a mortar, baked it and the taste of it was like fresh oil. It is the seed that they gathered, beat in the mortar, cooked and ate that had the taste of fresh anointing. The Psalmist said, *'I shall be anointed with fresh oil'* (Psalm 92:10). Jesus himself said:

> *It is written, Man shall not live by bread alone, but by every word that proceedeth out of the mouth of God.*
>
> MATTHEW 4:4

In other words, just like bread feeds the physical body, the Word of God is spirit food to the spirit of man.

Meditation – This means the musing upon, muttering of, rehearsing and storing of the Word of God in your spirit and mind. It is Word-thought repetition transfusing the Scripture throughout the texture of the spirit and soul. Constantly meditate upon the Logos so that it can become a Rhema, speaking back to you when you need it. One day, you may hear a negative report or step into a situation and suddenly a scripture verse pops in your mind. What is this? It's a *quickened* Word, a Rhema, a trigger point that you need to defeat the circumstance.

Once again as a reminder, Solomon said: *'The spirit of man is the candle of the Lord, **searching all the inward parts** of the belly.'* (Proverbs 20:27). Your spirit man is looking for something! What is your spirit looking for? It's looking for a Word that will deal directly with the present circumstance. What if there is no Word there? Then you are going to be in a world of trouble. This is pretty much like a computer or laptop, with so many files, emails and documents in it. What if a situation arises and I need to look for a particular document that I cannot find. What do I do? On my MacBook Air, I simply go to the Spotlight Search, type the title of the document and what is found in the computer shows up. Different computers have slightly different search mechanisms but they do have one, a place where you type in the title of the document that you need, press 'search' and wait while your computer looks for the particular file. Once it is done, it might say, 'six files found ' with the title you are looking for. If there are no such files, it will say, 'zero files found'. This is pretty much how your spirit operates. It is looking for a promise-file to counteract and defeat your problem. However for so many believers, due to their meditating on the things of the world and not the Word, what comes up is 'zero promises found'. This is not a place to find yourself in.

Meditation is deliberately planting the seeds of God's thoughts in the bed of your heart and letting them grow in your conscious and subconscious mind. A great example of what meditation is can be understood by observing the cow chewing the cud. The dictionary defines cud as 'that portion of food which is brought up by ruminating animals from their first stomach to be chewed a second time'. Take a Scripture verse and muse upon it for ten minutes, to all day long if you choose and let it speak back to you. Let that Scripture soak through your conscious and subconsciousness. Just like a cow has one stomach with four different parts or chambers, meditation is digesting the Word in the different chambers of your make up – your mouth, mind and spirit. In meditation,the Word goes into the chamber of your mouth to the chamber of your mind and the chamber of your spirit to later being regurgitated from your spirit to your mind then through your mouth to have an effect upon your body, emotions and circumstance. Whatever you program into your heart is what will eventually come out of your mouth.

Meditation is deliberately planting the seeds of God's thoughts in the bed of your heart and letting them grow in your conscious and subconscious mind

---

Scripture Confessions – After chewing upon and meditating on the Word, it becomes important for you to speak it out. You cannot change any situation without speaking. This is the law of faith and dominion in the earth. Confession is *homologeo* in Greek, meaning to '*say the same thing*'. Hence Scripture confession is saying the same thing that the Scripture says about your circumstance. Your faith is triggered or released by your confession and it is another way of feeding your spirit.

> *A man's belly shall be satisfied with the fruit of his mouth; and with the increase of his lips shall he be filled. Death and life are in the power of the tongue: and they that love it shall eat the fruit thereof.*
>
> PROVERBS 18:20, 21

The man's *belly* here is referring to his spirit man and it will be satisfied by the words of his mouth, either words of life or words of death. The words of your mouth feed and condition your spirit and renew your mind. A man's natural belly is satisfied by the food in his mouth and a man's spirit is satisfied by the Word-food in his mouth. This is why confession is partaking of spirit food. The more you speak God's Word, the more you are feeding your spirit.

Eye and Ear gate – Another way that you also feed your spirit man is through your eye and ear gate. This is why you must be protective over what comes into your ears and before your eyes.

> *My son, attend to my words; **incline thine ear** unto my sayings. Let them **not depart from thine eyes;** keep them in the midst of thine heart. For they are life unto those that find them, and health to all their flesh. Keep thy heart with all diligence; for out of it are the issues of life. Put away from thee a froward mouth, and perverse lips put far from thee. Let thine eyes look right on, and let thine eyelids look straight before thee.*
>
> PROVERBS 4:20-25

The Word must be constantly be in your eyes and ears to activate the law of receiving, which Solomon unveiled in Proverbs. Your eyes, ears and mouth are the feeding mechanism to your spirit.

---

*Your eyes, ears and mouth are
feeding mechanisms to your spirit*

ꝺ Drinking Habits

Your drinking habits must also change. Do not drink the Kool-aid of Satan's unbelief and fear but be drunk on the wine of the Spirit. Drinking of the new wine of the Spirit is the exact tonic that your spirit man needs daily. Drink of the rivers of living water. Stop drinking from the media. By now you must realize that the media is the fear machine of Satan, created to paralyze your faith and have crippling effects on your spirit.

ꝺ Join a good church and have a good pastor

Secondly, another way of developing a great physique is that you need to join a good gym with great facilities to work out your whole body. This means you have to go to a good church. What is a good church? This is a great question which so many people fail to answer correctly:

❯ The make up of a good church

Most would say a great church is one that is close to them, has great music and great facilities. For most people it is more of a visual thing than a spiritual thing. While having a good building is important it is not the most essential thing. The idea that a church is good because it is close by is as repulsive as saying you eat out of a trashcan because it happens to be close by. A good church is one which:

* Feeds you spiritually with the Word, not seeker friendly pablum;
* Renews your mind mentally;

❖ Challenges your prayer life;

❖ Equips your children spiritually;

❖ Equips you as a soldier of the Lord;

❖ Builds your faith;

❖ Enhances your relationship with the Lord.

〉 Have a good pastor

People in the sport world use a good trainer or coach to bring out the best in them. The coach can see your mistakes and help to correct them. The coach or trainer is not your best friend but is there to make sure that you reach your potential. This is what you need in a pastor. They are not here to be your best friend or to make you laugh. They are here to train you spiritually and make a giant out of you.

〉 What makes a good pastor?

❖ They feed you the un-compromised word of God;

❖ They create an environment for you to growth;

❖ They challenge you to be the believer that you were meant to be;

❖ They stretch your faith;

❖ They love you enough to tell you of your shortcomings;

❖ They push you beyond your limits.

⑨ Exercise-Workout routine

Without exercise or work outs, you will not build a strong physique. In the same manner, you will need to exercise and work out in order to build a strong spiritual physique. Here are seven exercises you need to implement in order to build and fine-tune your spirit.

1 BE A HEARER AND A DOER OF THE WORD.

Acting on the Word is the exercise that will build your muscles spiritually. To just be a hearer and not a doer of the Word is to be self-deceived. Be quick to act upon the Word of God. The quicker you are to act upon the Word, the stronger you will be spiritually. The supernatural is unleashed the moment you act on the Word, as heaven will back you up the moment you decide to take God at His Word. Be a hearer *and* a doer. You will become a doer when you become a hearer. This is why you constantly need to be hearing God's word. How do we hear God's Word?

* Reading and studying his Word;
* Listen to audio bible on-line, on your phone or CDs;
* Attend services to hear a good strong Word;
* Listen to preaching and teaching constantly. Turn your car into a spiritual university rather than listening to garbage from the radio.

2 PRAY IN TONGUES CONSTANTLY AND PRAY THE WORD

This is a master key to building a strong spirit. *'But ye, beloved, building up yourselves on your most holy faith, praying in the Holy Ghost'* (Jude 1:20). Praying in tongues is erecting a strong edifice. It will give your spirit man the ascendancy over your flesh, opening you up to the divine mysteries that God has for you. I pray in the spirit as much as I can and for as long as I can. This is a daily affair for me. It should be for you too. It will stretch the capacity of your spirit to believe for more, to receive more and experience more of God. The enlargement of your spirit – as you pray in tongues – will be the building of a strong spiritual life that will be a benefit to your generation.

One of the greatest men of God in the twentieth century was John G. Lake. He experienced some terrible times in his life, nonetheless he was a conqueror. What was the secret to John G. Lake's life and ministry? Let Mr Lake tell you in his own words: *'I want to talk with the utmost frankness and say to you, **that tongues have been the making of my ministry**. It is that* *peculiar communication with God when God reveals to my soul the truth I utter to you day by day in the ministry... Many times, I climb out of bed, take my pencil and pad, and jot down the beautiful things of God, the wonderful things of God that He talks out in my spirit and reveals to my heart.'* Please pay attention to these words: 'Tongues have been the making of my ministry.'

Another great giant of faith who knew the power of praying in tongues constantly was Smith Wigglesworth. According to secular standards, he was an uneducated plumber who, after he received the baptism of tongues, was radically transformed into an apostle of faith. The miracles, boldness, and manifestation of the supernatural became evident in his life and ministry. Here are his own words, an excerpt from his great book:

> *'We must be edified before we can edify the church. **I cannot estimate what I, personally, owe to the Holy Ghost method of spiritual edification.** I am here before you as one of the biggest conundrums in the world. There never was a weaker man on the platform. Language? None. Inability – full of it. All natural things in my life point exactly opposite to my being able to stand on the platform and preach the gospel. The secret is that the Holy Ghost came and brought this wonderful edification of the Spirit. **I had been reading this Word continually as well as I could, but the Holy Ghost came and took hold of it, for the Holy Ghost is the breath of it, and He illuminated it to me.** And He gives me language that I cannot speak fast enough; it comes too fast; and it is there because God has given it. When the Comforter is come He shall teach you ALL things; and He has given me this supernatural means of speaking in an unknown tongue to edify myself, so that, after being edified, I can edify the church...'*
>
> EVER INCREASING FAITH – SMITH WIGGLESWORTH

The more you pray in tongues the more you are charging and recharging your spiritual battery. Make it a daily affair! Your spirit man will soar in the place of intense praying in the spirit.

Give yourself to much prayers. In fact Paul told the Colossians:

Continue in prayer, and watch in the same with thanksgiving;
COLOSSIANS 4:2

Devote yourselves to prayer with an alert mind and a thankful heart.
NEW LIVING TRANSLATION

Keep praying. Pay attention when you offer prayers of thanksgiving.
GOD'S WORD® TRANSLATION

It is inconceivable to give yourself to a long stretch of hours praying in tongues yet your spirit man remains undeveloped; when you devote yourself to long stretches of time praying in tongues it will add to the weight of glory that you carry and the quality of the impact or impartation you can make in people's lives. Empty vessels cannot impart into people. Now you can understand why Paul said to the Romans: 'For I long to see you, that I may impart unto you some spiritual gift, to the end ye may be established.' (Romans 1:11). To impart is to transmit and communicate something tangible from one's inner man to another's inner or outer man. This is where praying in tongues takes center-stage. That is the reason why Paul was thankful that he prayed in tongues more than anyone among his contemporaries. This is quite a statement when you consider who his peers were.

Giving yourself to long stretch of time of praying in tongues will add to the weight of glory that you can carry and impart in people's lives

---

Tongues is a face to face encounter with God. Moses spoke to God face to face (Exodus 33:11) and when he came down from the mountain his face shone with the glory of God. Paul said that when we pray in tongues we are speaking directly to God. Tongues is your access to the glory of God. If you want to be a heavy-weight in the spirit, like the apostle Paul and Moses, it is imperative that you dedicate yourself to a life of praying in tongues.

You cannot go beyond your level of your own prayer life. I have spent thousands of hours – since I was fourteen – praying in the spirit. I know the virtues and values it will add to your life. I am not speaking to you about a theory. For me, like the apostle Paul, I want to say, *'I thank my God that I speak in tongues more than ye all.'* (1 Corinthians 14:18). I have prayed for the unknown and for my destiny for hours in tongues. I can safely tell you that my life has been the better for it. Praying in tongues is how you generate power, release power, activate favor, attract grace, attack circumstances, accelerate protection and secure provision from God.

Praying in tongues is how you generate power, release power, activate favor, attract grace, attack circumstances, accelerate protection and secure provision from God

---

Furthermore as it pertains to praying, especially praying with your understanding, the best kind of prayer is when you pray the Word back to God. God loves it when you send his Word back to Him. God always keeps His Word. Jesus said, *'The Scripture cannot be broken.'* (John 10:35). Always remember this: God is not obligated to keep your Word but He is obligated to keep His Word:

*For when God made promise to Abraham, because he could swear by no greater, he sware by himself, Saying, Surely blessing I will bless thee, and multiplying I will multiply thee. And so, after he had patiently endured, he obtained the promise. For men verily swear by the greater: and **an oath for confirmation is to them an end of all strife**. Wherein God, willing more abundantly to shew unto the heirs of promise the **immutability of his counsel, confirmed it by an oath**: That by **two immutable things**, in which it was impossible for God to lie, we might have a strong consolation, who have fled for refuge to lay hold upon the hope set before us.*

HEBREWS 6:13-18

The two immutable and unchangeable things are God's Word and God's oath. He did not have to swear but He did it for our benefit. God's Word is good by itself but He took an oath for our mind to be at rest. Notice what Hebrews injected: '*an oath for confirmation is to them an end of all strife.*' (Hebrews 6:16). Some translations say: 'an oath ends all arguments, unbelief, doubts and disputes' and another one says: 'And without any question that oath is binding'. God has bound Himself to His Word and His oath and we have strong consolation because of that. The patriarch, Job, who went through a period of great trials, said: '*Surely I would speak to the Almighty, and I desire to reason with God.*' (Job 13:3). This is exactly what we are doing when we pray the Word of God back to Him. We are reasoning with God. Taking God's promise in your mouth and praying it back to Him will be your pathway to answered prayer. One thing is for sure, there will not be an ounce of unbelief if you pray the Word back to God.

3 ALWAYS WALK THE LOVE WALK.

When you became born again, the love of God was shed abroad in your heart by the Holy Spirit. Therefore the God kind of love is resident within you. The God kind of love is compassionate, quick to forgive and tender-hearted. Notice I said 'tender-hearted' and not 'hard-hearted'. When you walk in love, you will have a tender heart toward others and a tender heart towards God. Love has no room for bitterness, strife and revilings. Since God's love is kind and tender-hearted, it is always ready to forgive. It does not procrastinate forgiveness or linger in bitterness. When you walk the love walk, it makes your faith effective. Paul said to the Ephesians: '*And be ye kind one to another, tenderhearted, **forgiving one another** even as God for Christ's sake hath forgiven you.*' (Ephesians 4:32). See, these words, 'Forgiving one another' have no stipulations attached. This simply means you have to forgive them even when you feel they are undeserved and whether you feel like it or not. It did not say 'forgive them when they start walking right.' No! Simply just forgive. Why? Because God forgave you without stipulations and every time you go to God for forgiveness, He simply forgives. So make sure that you do not allow a root of bitterness in your heart.

Looking diligently lest any man fail of the grace of God; lest any root of bitterness springing up trouble you, and thereby many be defiled.
                                                              HEBREWS 12:15

Bitterness is a root that grows into a tree of trouble whose leaves will defile you. Walking in love undergirds your faith to secure victory in life. So be quick to repent, quick to forgive.

Bitterness is a root that grows into a tree of trouble whose leaves will defile you

---

4 GIVE YOURSELF TO REGULAR FASTING.

Fasting is a great form of discipline, giving your spirit ascendency over your flesh.

As in physical muscle-building, which begins with the tearing down of existing muscle tissue, fasting is the process of tearing down the flesh to build the spirit. Your flesh will be the biggest obstacle in your spiritual life. As long as your flesh is strong (meaning dictating your life) that's the weakest that you will ever be. The weaker your flesh is (meaning that you follow the dictates of your spirit), the more you will be at the peak of your strength. Fasting helps you in your resistance capacity. If you cannot resist food, how will you resist the devil? Therefore fasting is the subduing of your flesh, revealing your consistent leaning upon God. Fasting is a great way to stretch your spirit, soul and body.

From today I want you to see fasting as a great launching pad for muscle-building for your spirit. There are many who would love to be spiritually big but cannot stop from physical feasting. The Psalmist, listing some benefits of the anointing, uttered these words: '*But my horn shalt thou exalt like the horn of a unicorn: I shall be anointed with fresh oil... They shall still bring forth fruit in old age; they shall be fat and flourishing.*' (Psalm 92:10, 14).

Notice the connection between fresh anointing oil with flourishing and fatness. The Hebrew word for 'fat' is 'dashen', meaning 'to be rich and fertile'. Flourishing in Hebrew is 'ra'anan' meaning 'to be green and leafy'. To be spiritually fat means that you are expressing the anointing, and can impart it into the lives of others. It means that when people leave your presence they have had an encounter with God and are satisfied. Have you ever been to a church service or convention, or been to see an evangelist with your expectation level high, only to come home disappointed? Certainly! Why? Because the person who ministered was lean spiritually. As a believer or minister, are you spiritually lean or spiritually fat?

In the world, people who are rich, feast physically but are spiritually deficient. When it comes to the things of God, those who will have great spiritual feasts will be those who fast. I love this Scripture from the mouth of Paul: *'For which cause we faint not; but though our outward man perish, yet the inward man is renewed day by day.'* (2 Corinthians 4:16). Fasting is deliberately weakening the flesh in order to strengthen the spirit. David uttered these powerful thoughts to us in his Psalm to God:

> *O God, thou art my God; early will I seek thee: my soul thirsteth for thee,*
> *my flesh longeth for thee in a dry and thirsty land, where no water is;*
> *To see thy power and thy glory, so as I have seen thee in the sanctuary.*
>   Psalm 63:1, 2

If you want to see God's power and glory you must seek Him. David said to God: 'Early will I seek you, my soul and my flesh long for you.' Fasting is seeking God, causing your soul to feast upon Him. Denial of the flesh is the renewal of the spirit. Physical leanness will provoke spiritual fitness. Paul told us to 'present our bodies as a living sacrifice' and we know when God accepted sacrifices, He honored it by fire. When we fast, we are presenting our bodies as living sacrifices and God will honor your sacrifice with His fire. If you want to get fitter and bigger spiritually then you must engage more in fasting. To spiritually impact people, you must be spiritually fat. Be a lightweight physically and you will be a heavyweight spiritually!

An important point to stress – Use wisdom with an understanding of your physical makeup before you start fasting. If you have not fasted for one day, it is pointless for you to shoot for a forty day fast. Train yourself little by little. Don't get all emotionally psyched up to go for a long fast right out the gate. You must realize that you will have to deal with detoxing issues, which can be very uncomfortable and painful. The quest of fasting is to shut down carnal voices and stretch your spirit to be sensitive to God. Some people through a lack of wisdom have done serious damage to themselves when it comes to fasting. Train yourself in fasting. Fast half a day and learn something from it. Fast a day and learn something from it. Take it a step at a time.

5 FOLLOW THE INSTRUCTION THAT IS IMPRESSED UPON YOUR HEART.

Learn to follow and act upon the inner impression. As you spend much time in the Word and praying in tongues, you will become more sensitive to His promptings. If you start to recognize the inner promptings of the Spirit and act upon them, after a while you will become more accustomed to His leading. The more that you do this, the more confident and conversant you will be with the Holy Spirit. Learn to trust God in small things to be familiar with His voice in order for you to trust to hear His voice in big situations. Once you know and sense His promptings, act upon them quickly. The more you do the more you are exercising your spirit.

Trust God from the bottom of your heart; don't try to figure out everything on your own. ***Listen for God's voice in everything you do, everywhere you go;*** *he's the one who will keep you on track.*
                    PROVERBS 3: 5-7 MESSAGE TRANSLATION

6 CONFESS THE WORD

At the beginning, Christianity was called the Great Confession. It is still the Great Confession and the quicker you realize this then the quicker you will watch what comes out of your mouth. According to Job, words have forces behind them (Job 6:25). Words are carriers and containers. Once you are aware of the power of words you will be like David who said: '*Set a watch, O Lord, before my mouth; keep the door of my lips.*' (Psalm 141:3). Paul said to the Romans: '*Confession is made unto salvation*' (Romans 10:10). Literally this verse should read as, 'Confession constitutes your salvation.' Just as the founding fathers of America wrote and signed the Constitution and the Declaration of Independence, your confession will be the constitution of your life, signed by your tongue. Confession is *homologeo* in Greek and it means 'to say the same word'. Therefore confession simply means to say the same word that God has already said about your situation.

Just as the founding fathers of America wrote and signed the Constitution and Declaration of Independence, your confession will be the constitution of your life signed by your tongue

---

In order to be initiated into the Christian faith it was imperative for you to confess the Lordship of Christ over your life, taking you out of hell and into heaven. But beyond your initial confession, you need to learn the secret of continual confession that enables mastery over the devil and life's circumstances. Let me emphasize some facts between *initial* and *continual* confession:

❖ Your initial confession enabled the Lordship of Christ in and over your life;
   You continual confession enables your mastery in Christ over the world the flesh and the devil.

❖ Your initial confession took you out of hell and into heaven;
   Your continual confession brings heaven onto the earth.

❖ Your initial confession allowed the impartation of the divine nature in your spirit;
   Your continual confession allows the expression of the divine nature in your spirit.

❖ Your initial confession made you the righteousness of God;
Your continual confession establishes the righteousness of God in you.

❖ Your initial confession confirmed Christ in you;
Your continual confession confirms you in Christ.

❖ Your initial confession confirmed your confession of Christ before the Father;
Your continual confession confirms Christ's confession of you before the Father.

Therefore one of the greatest exercises that you can do to build a strong spirit is confess the Word. Confessing who you are in Christ is a sure way to build a strong spirit and create a strong base of operations for your life. This is what Paul told Philemon:

That the communication of thy faith may become effectual by the acknowledging of every good thing which is in you in Christ Jesus.
PHILEMON 1:6

Your faith becomes energized when you acknowledge and confess who you are in Christ. Your spirit will soar as you keep confessing your redemption in Christ. Acknowledging your positional truth in Christ enables you to master the world, the flesh and the devil. Always remember that your faith will never rise above your level of confession. This is why confession is a great training technique.

Wherefore, holy brethren, partakers of the heavenly calling, consider the Apostle and High Priest of our profession, Christ Jesus.
HEBREWS 3:1

The greatest fight you will ever face is the fight to maintain and keep your confession. In the midst of trials and testings the temptation is to let go of what you know to be the truth of God's Word. This is why the author of Hebrews tells us: '*Let us hold fast the profession of our faith without wavering;*

(for he is faithful that promised).' (Hebrews 10:23). Jesus is your advocate, meaning He is your defense attorney: He is the executor of your confession. The way He defends you is by your confession. In fact the Lord Jesus himself maintained a good confession before Pilate while He was being accused and beaten. You need to hold onto your confession in the midst of troubles and trials. On a daily basis you need to:

❖ Confess your redemption in Christ;
❖ Confess the realities of the New Creation;
❖ Confess the 'in him', 'in whom' and 'in Christ' realities;
❖ Confess your covenant in Christ above the curses in the world.

7 Memorial place

Altars and places of memorial were mentioned over and over in the Bible. An altar was a monument built to connect with the supernatural and commemorate a divine occurrence which took place at a certain location. In bible days, altars were very significant, indicating communion with God, a place of worship and a covenant memorial. Today we do not have to erect altars but we can still have places of covenant memorial: this could be your prayer room or any other place that you have chosen to connect with God. The point being whenever you step into that place, you keep connecting with God. For me, apart from my Holy Room in my house designated for prayer only, I have developed the habit that as soon as I step into the shower and the water hits my head, confession of who I am in Christ comes out. Since I shower everyday, I confess daily. I also take my dog on a walk in the woods when I am home from my travels. So whenever I step in the woods, I begin to confess the Word, pray in tongues and praise the Lord. For you it might be on your way to work in the car. If so, use that time to confess who you are in Christ. Implement into your routine daily, the habit of confessing your position and inheritance in Christ. This will definitely be the building of your spirit man.

8 CARDIO VASCULAR EXERCISES

One of the greatest things you can do for your body is called Cardio vascular exercises. This includes walking and running to pump your heart rate to keep the blood flowing and for you to lose the excess weight you may be carrying. Walking and running are great for the health of your heart. Protecting your heart is a great way to great health. This corresponds perfectly to what the book of Proverbs tells us:

Keep thy heart with all diligence; for out of it are the issues of life.

PROVERBS 4:23

So how is this applicable to our lives?

We need to apply the same thing spiritually that we do physically. In order to keep a healthy heart, we need to:

❖ Walk by faith:

For we walk by faith, not by sight.

2 CORINTHIANS 5:7

❖ Walk in love:

And walk in love, as Christ also hath loved us, and hath given himself for us an offering and a sacrifice to God for a sweetsmelling savour.

EPHESIANS 5:2

❖ Walk honestly:

Let us walk honestly, as in the day; not in rioting and drunkenness, not in chambering and wantonness, not in strife and envying.

ROMANS 13:13

❖ Walk circumspectly:

See then that ye walk circumspectly, not as fools, but as wise.

EPHESIANS 5:15

❖ Walk in wisdom:

Walk in wisdom toward them that are without, redeeming the time.

COLOSSIANS 4:5

❖ Walk in the Spirit:

This I say then, Walk in the Spirit, and ye shall not fulfil the lust of the flesh

GALATIANS 5:16

❖ Walk worthy of the Lord:

That ye might walk worthy of the Lord unto all pleasing, being fruitful in every good work, and increasing in the knowledge of God.

COLOSSIANS 1:10

❖ Walk in the light:

But if we walk in the light, as he is in the light, we have fellowship one with another, and the blood of Jesus Christ his Son cleanseth us from all sin.

1 JOHN 1:7

❖ Walk in the truth:

I have no greater joy than to hear that my children walk in truth.

3 JOHN 4

❖ Run with patience:

Wherefore seeing we also are compassed about with so great a cloud of witnesses, let us lay aside every weight, and the sin which doth so easily beset us, and let us run with patience the race that is set before us

HEBREWS 12:1

Walking and running will keep your heart healthy. Make sure that you do not allow the cares of this world, the deceitfulness of riches and the lust of other things to enter into your heart. If you do, they will choke the Word. Keep your heart free from envy, jealousy, bitterness and other negativity, in order to keep the life of God continually flowing from it.

CHAPTER 9
TRAINING THE HUMAN SPIRIT – *PART 2*

W E have been looking at how to train and build your human spirit by having a parallel look at a man who is purposely endeavoring to build his body physically. We have looked at the exercises and now we want to have a quick look at the following four remaining acts you must implement in order for you to train and build your spirit man to hit its potential.

1 HAVE A PARTNER TO MOTIVATE

Iron sharpeneth iron; so a man sharpeneth the countenance of his friend."
                                                             PROVERBS 27:17

There is an old adage that says, 'Birds of a feather flock together.' One of the best ways to develop a strong spirit is to hang around someone who has a strong spirit. You have seen it when you go to the gym, two friends working out together and pushing one another to be better. We all need friends that will push us and remind us that we can do more and be better. I am sure you have heard this saying, 'My best friend is the one that brings the best out of me.' The Scripture is clear that one will put a thousand to flight but two will chase ten thousand (Deuteronomy 32:30). Do you remember when Peter and John were threatened by the religious leaders after the healing of the impotent man at the Gate called Beautiful in Acts 3? After being threatened, the Scripture tells us: '*And being let go, they went to their own company...*' (Acts 4:23). It is good to be in the company of people that have things in common with us. Going back to their company, they prayed again together and the place was shaken with them being emboldened by the Holy Spirit. Iron does sharpen iron.

I like Matthew Poole's commentary on this verse:

Iron cutting tools are made bright, and sharp, and fit for use by rubbing them against the file, or some other iron. So a man, who being alone is sad, and dull, and unactive, by the company and conversation of his friend is greatly refreshed, his very wits are sharpened, and his spirit revived, and he is both fitted for and provoked to action.

The countenance is here put for the mind or spirit, whose temper or disposition is commonly visible in men's countenances.

MATTHEW POOLE COMMENTARY

We all need that friend with the spirit of faith that challenges us to believe God for great things. There are people that you meet and when you leave them you have a sense of the greatness of God. On the other hand there are other people that after you leave them, all you sense is the size of your problem. You do not need to be hanging around this kind of person. They will only sap the strength from your spirit. David's men became mighty men who did great feats but they did not start out like that:

*David therefore departed thence, and escaped to the cave Adullam: and when his brethren and all his father's house heard it, they went **down** thither to him. And every one that was in distress, and every one that was **in debt**, and every one that was **discontented**, gathered themselves unto him; and he became a captain over them: and there were with him about four hundred men.*

1 SAMUEL 22:1-2

David became a captain over 400 men who came down to him in distress, in debt and discontented. How would you like to have an army of men like these guys? However that did not bother David because he had the spirit of faith. He had that giant-killing anointing upon him which was transferred to these 400 men as they connected with him. You become like those you spend time with.

*Make no friendship with an angry man; and with a furious man thou
shalt not go: Lest thou learn his ways, and get a snare to thy soul.*
PROVERBS 22:24-25

*Don't hang out with angry people; don't keep company with hotheads.
Bad temper is contagious – don't get infected.*
MESSAGE TRANSLATION

Those in your inner circle will either infect you with unbelief or inspire
you with faith. The people in your life can be iron-sharpening or they can
be lead-poisoning. Paul had some great people in his life:

*I beseech you, brethren, (ye know the house of Stephanas, that it is
the firstfruits of Achaia, and that they have addicted themselves to the
ministry of the saints, That ye submit yourselves unto such, and to every
one that helpeth with us, and laboureth.*
1 CORINTHIANS 16:15-16

The people in the life of Paul were those who were addicted to ministry.
They were helpers of his ministry and they were great laborers for the
kingdom of God. Paul had more to say in regards to these people:

*I am glad of the coming of Stephanas and Fortunatus and Achaicus: **for
that which was lacking on your part they have supplied. For they have
refreshed my spirit and yours:** therefore acknowledge ye them that are
such.*
1 CORINTHIANS 16:17-18)

In Romans 16, Paul gives us a litany of people who were of great help
to him:

Phoebe, *a dear Christian woman from the town of Cenchreae, will
be coming to see you soon.* **She has worked hard in the church there.**

*Receive her as your sister in the Lord, giving her a warm Christian welcome. Help her in every way you can, **for she has helped many in their needs, including me.** Tell **Priscilla and Aquila** hello. They have been **my fellow workers in the affairs of Christ Jesus. In fact, they risked their lives for me,** and I am not the only one who is thankful to them; so are all the Gentile churches.*

*Please give my greetings to all those who meet to worship in their home. Greet my good friend Epaenetus. He was the very first person to become a Christian in Asia. **Remember me to Mary, too, who has worked so hard to help us.** Then there are **Andronicus and Junias, my relatives who were in prison with me.** They are respected by the apostles and became Christians before I did. Please give them my greetings. Say hello to Ampliatus, whom I love as one of God's own children, 9 and Urbanus, our fellow worker, and beloved Stachys.*

*Then there is Apelles, a good man whom the Lord approves; greet him for me. And give my best regards to those **working at the house of Aristobulus.** Remember me to Herodion my relative. Remember me to the Christian slaves over at Narcissus House. Say hello to **Tryphaena and Tryphosa, the Lord's workers, and to dear Persis, who has worked so hard for the Lord. Greet Rufus for me, whom the Lord picked out to be his very own; and also his dear mother who has been such a mother to me.***

Romans 16:1-13

It is written that the Pharisees and the religious leaders of the day took note of the disciples after the miracle of the impotent man at the gate called Beautiful:

Now when they saw the boldness of Peter and John, and perceived that they were unlearned and ignorant men, they marvelled; and they took knowledge of them, that they had been with Jesus.

Acts 4:13

Being with Jesus! Spending time with Jesus gave the disciples the mannerisms and character of Jesus. This is why in your quest to build a great spiritual physique make it your top priority to spend time with people who build your faith rather than build unbelief in you.

2 TAKE SUPPLEMENTS

When you look at people who are serious at building their physiques, one thing is for sure: they take supplements. By supplements I am talking about vitamins, protein shakes and other products to aid them in achieving their goals. The same things will apply to you.

Apart from daily feeding upon the milk, bread, meat and strong meat of the Word and drinking from the river of the Holy Spirit, you will also need daily supplements to assist you, but realize that supplements cannot take the place of your daily food and drink: they are to assist you in your goals. What would be the supplements for you and I? Here are the supplements that assist me in my goals:

❖ Book reading;
❖ Audio or Mp3 messages;
❖ Magazines;
❖ DVD and Mp4 messages;
❖ Conventions;
❖ Seminars.

Books and messages are my daily supplement. I look for the best information and digest them daily. I remember when I was younger how I would compete with myself on a daily and weekly basis to see how many books or magazine articles I could read and how many messages I could listen to or watch, as well as taking notes. I can tell you that these actions have been the making of my life. I remember one long weekend I purposely stayed in the house and listened to over twenty five messages. I got up before 8am and just went at it until I had that 25 messages in my spirit. That weekend I had listened to Kenneth Copeland, Kenneth Hagin, Frederick K C Price and Mike Murdock.

I also made it a point to attend as many conventions as I could from the time I was a teenager. I went to a K.C.M. Believers' Convention where there were meetings all day long for six days. Although my body was physically tired my spirit was charged. I felt like Superman. From the time I was 15 years old I went to bed listening to preaching and teaching and left it on through the night. I have been doing this for years now. People have asked me, 'How can you sleep with all that noise blaring? I couldn't sleep with somonee constantly jabbering!' My answer has always been the same: 'I don't know how someone can go to bed without listening to the Word. I sleep very well, with no worries.' So make sure you get your supplement.

3 REST

This was a very hard lesson for me to learn. I am a person who is on the move all the time; I hate not maximizing my day. I have been accused of being a workaholic and that is a badge that I have gladly worn. I do not think a lot of people can keep up with my pace. I frustrate people who work with me as I have work on my mind all the time; I don't switch off; once a project is done, I move on to the next. I fly constantly and on the plane I am working, writing books. I do not sit on a plane and say to myself, 'Wow, I have a twelve hour flight, so I can watch 6 movies.' No way! My thought is , 'I have twelves hours, nobody knows me on the plane and no one will disturb me therefore I can write a manuscript during the flight.' This portion that you are reading is being written after an eleven hour flight from Atlanta to Lagos and being stuck in traffic for four hours on my way to another city called Ibadan in Nigeria. When I want something done, it gets done, no matter what. I have pushed my body with work to extremities which were not healthy. There was a time I thought that sleep was just a waste of time. Even till today, I don't like to go to sleep but once I go to sleep I don't like to get up. I get very few hours of sleep because to me in the hours that one sleeps one can do a lot of things. I got my work ethics from my dad. He would work hard as a gourmet chef in a French restaurant in Central London and his hours would be 11am – 3:00pm and then be back home at 4pm only to leave again at 5 pm back to the same restaurant till 11:30 pm. Many times my dad would be back home after 1am and I would watch him drink black coffee. So I could not wait to get to the age when I could drink black coffee and work round the clock. Remember how I told you how I used to compete with myself to see how many messages and books I can read in a week? When I was young, I was working in a clothing shop as a manager. I remember one particular week, I was at work from 9am till 6pm (as usual) but that evening, instead of resting and going to sleep I would just be reading, studying, praying (all good things) and drinking coffee, not getting any sleep. I did this for four days and by the evening of the fifth day, my body just gave up on me: I was feeling sick and violently throwing up; I was in bad shape for a few days. It was not the devil attacking me, but me attacking my own body by refusing to rest, which God, Himself, ordained for our benefit. Sometimes there is no need for the devil to attack us, we attack ourselves by our lack of wisdom! You can't keep the pedal to the metal without braking and not expect an accident or something to go wrong. We can get so busy that we wear ourselves out.

Resting is not laziness but replenishment for your well being. Even Jesus needed to rest.

Now Jacob's well was there. Jesus therefore, being wearied with his journey, sat thus on the well: and it was about the sixth hour.

JOHN 4:6

Many years ago, the man of God, Dr Mike Murdock made this statement: '*Faith walks out when fatigue walks in.*' That statement set me free! Please pay attention to the effects of weariness and not resting:

* Weariness stops you from operating at your optimum level;
* Weariness makes you irritable, impatient and is the cause of impulsive decisions that you will likely regret later;
* Weariness causes you to say things that you would never say normally that bring hurt to your loved ones;
* Weariness clouds your thinking;
* Weariness kills your passion and focus;
* Weariness attracts diseases;
* Weariness stops the best in you and brings the worst out of you;
* Weariness and not resting will bring you to place of sin.

Look at the recommendation of Jesus to his disciples after they came back from an extensive preaching trip:

> *And he said unto them, Come ye yourselves apart into a desert place, and rest a while: for there were many coming and going, and they had no leisure so much as to eat.*
>
> MARK 6:31

Those words are striking! 'Be apart by yourself in a desert place and rest a while.' There was so much going on, many comings and goings that they did not even have time to eat. Sometimes life can feel like this. I know ministry can feel like this! The words that are also striking are, 'they had no leisure'. This is where many people are and certainly where many ministers are. For many ministers and people, 'leisure' is viewed as a sin against God but in reality the lack of it is sin against our own body. To be honest, it is a sin of pride, thinking we are superman. However the Lord said, 'Come ye yourselves apart into a desert place and rest for a while'.

4 BALANCING THE NATURAL AND SPIRITUAL

God loves balance and that is why He gave you two legs. '*A false balance is an abomination before the Lord*' according to Proverbs 11:1. Some people feel that life is all spiritual and there can be no fun in the natural. Now when I say fun, I do not mean engaging in the sins and pleasures of the world: I am talking about rest and relaxation. Resting is not laziness but allowing your spirit, soul and body time to replenish. You need to learn that! I needed to learn that! Even people who are heavy into body building know to rest their muscles the following day and work a different part of their body. The resting allows the muscles that have been torn to rebuild and be bigger. Here are some benefits of rest:

❖ It gives you time to **reflect;**
❖ It gives you time to **rebuild;**
❖ It gives you time to **refocus;**
❖ It gives time to **reactivate** energy and **reignites** passion;
❖ It gives time to **restore** health and vitality;
❖ It gives you time to make a **rational** decision.

There are times when I am back home in U.S. from a long trip and all I want to do is sit down watch some soccer, spend time with my family and walk or sit with my dog. This brings me so much relaxation. As much as I love reading books I enjoy reading my bible more. Reading the Scriptures is not a chore for me but my life. I love it! It energizes me! I remember after a particular long trip, my wife, my youngest daughter and I were in Florida for a few days, so we went to Disney World's Animal Kingdom. Just looking at the animals brought a sense of joy and then just being in the swimming pool, doing nothing but floating, reinvigorated my whole system. Floating upon the water and thinking upon scriptures with my eyes closed was wonderful. It was just a few days that replenished my life.

5 SOLITARY REFINEMENT

I want you to notice the words of Jesus: *'Come ye yourselves apart into a desert place and rest for a while'*. (Mark 6:31). It is not rest until you are apart in a desert place. What does that mean? Where are you going to find a desert when you live in a city? I am not referring to a physical desert but a quiet place where you can regroup and reload. With all the demands upon the ministry of Jesus, He kept going to the place of solitary refinement in the desert. Let us look at the instances when Jesus went into solitary refinement:

After the execution of his cousin, John the Baptist
*And his disciples came, and took up the body, and buried it, and went and told Jesus. When Jesus heard of it, **he departed thence by ship into a desert place apart:** and when the people had heard thereof, they followed him on foot out of the cities.*

MATTHEW 14:12-13

After great ministry demands
But he went out, and began to publish it much, and to blaze abroad the matter, insomuch that Jesus could no more openly enter into the city, but was without in desert places: and they came to him from every quarter."

MARK 1:45

After intense deliverance ministry in his own city
And came down to Capernaum, a city of Galilee, and taught them on the sabbath days... Now when the sun was setting, all they that had any sick with divers diseases brought them unto him; and he laid his hands on every one of them, and healed them. And devils also came out of many, crying out, and saying, Thou art Christ the Son of God. And he rebuking them suffered them not to speak: for they knew that he was Christ. And when it was day, he departed and went into a desert place: and the people sought him, and came unto him, and stayed him, that he should not depart from them.

LUKE 4:31, 40-42

🚩 **After his disciples mission trip**

And the apostles, when they were returned, told him all that they had done. And he took them, and went aside privately into a desert place belonging to the city called Bethsaida.

LUKE 9:10

You cannot keep unloading without reloading. You need to find yourself a private place and be apart, from all the business and busyness of your life. Sometimes it is just good to be away from your cell phone, laptop, iPad and television and give time to yourself to unwind. I call this private time *solitary refinement*, helping me to be a better person. For me that place is home because I am on the road all the time. Some people like fishing and for others it can simply be going for a walk or dining in a good restaurant. Whatever it is, make time for the things that you like. You need to make time for leisure. For me because I'm gone all the time, being home is a vacation for me. I just love being around my house and neighborhood. I also love the sea because I was born on a tropical island and I enjoy swimming in the sea. I love sitting on the beach and just listening to the sound of the sea, watching the sunset going down. It is relaxing to me. So at least once a year, I will have a few days swimming in the sea and go fishing with my brother, James, in Mauritius. He is famous for catching little fish and bragging about it. I also enjoy being with both of my brothers, winding them up about soccer and joking with them.

6 SPIRITUAL REFRESHING

For with stammering lips and another tongue will he speak to this people. To whom he said, This is the rest wherewith ye may cause the weary to rest; and this is the refreshing: yet they would not hear.

ISAIAH 28:11-12

...the times of refreshing shall come from the presence of the Lord.

ACTS 3:19

There is great revitalization when we spend time in the presence of the Lord in worship and praising His goodness. It will uplift your spirit and bring a sense of calm to you. Remember how when David played the harp, it would bing relief to Saul who was being attacked by a demon spirit? Choose the right worship to create an atmosphere of peace. His presence brings peace. His presence relieves stress. His presence shields you from the scorching and fiery darts of the wicked as you hide behind the great shield of faith. Isaiah in his book of prophecies told us this great truth:

> He giveth **power to the faint**; and to them that have no might he increaseth strength. Even the youths shall faint and be weary, and the young men shall utterly fall: **But they that wait upon the Lord shall renew their strength**; they shall mount up with wings as eagles; they shall run, and not be weary; and they shall walk, and not faint.
>
> ISAIAH 40:29-31

Waiting upon the Lord is both invigorating and revitalizing for your spirit man. Waiting upon the Lord is strength to your spirit man and your body. You will also notice in the life and ministry of Jesus the fact that He took time alone to be with His Father God. That is a great secret to being strengthened in spirit.

> But so much the more went there a fame abroad of him: and great multitudes came together to hear, and to be healed by him of their infirmities. And he withdrew himself into the wilderness, and prayed.
>
> LUKE 5:15-16

The secret to effective ministry is a revitalized and strengthened spirit. Real ministry is pouring out of the Spirit from your spirit man to another spirit man. Jesus knew this secret and Paul also knew this secret. That is why he said to the Ephesians:

*And be not drunk with wine, wherein is excess; **but be filled with the Spirit**; Speaking to yourselves in psalms and hymns and spiritual songs, singing and making melody in your heart to the Lord; Giving thanks always for all things unto God and the Father in the name of our Lord Jesus Christ.*
EPHESIANS 5:18-20

7 INITIAL AND CONTINUAL INFILLING

As per various Greek scholars and bible commentators, the words 'be filled with the Spirit' is in the Greek present imperative tense, connoting the idea of a *continuous replenishment*, an ongoing refilling. This verse is crudely and literally read as 'but be being filled with the Spirit'. In other words, 'keep on being filled constantly and continually.' You see there is the **initial** filling and the **continual** filling of the Holy Spirit. This is clearly played out in the early church where it says: '*And they were all filled with the Holy Ghost, and began to speak with other tongues, as the Spirit gave them utterance.*' (Acts 2:4). That was the **initial infilling** on the day of Pentecost. Then we see: '*And when they had prayed, the place was shaken where they were assembled together; and they were all filled with the Holy Ghost, and they spake the word of God with boldness.*'(Acts 4:31). This is continual infilling. The same disciples that received the initial infilling on the day of Pentecost received a **continual infilling** to speak the Word with boldness, with signs and wonders following. Among those who prayed and received the refilling were Peter and John. So how do we get this continuous filling and refilling?

▌ Prayer
And when they had prayed, the place was shaken...

ACTS 4:31

▌ Confession
Speaking to yourselves in psalms and hymns...

EPHESIANS 5:19

▌ Praise
Speaking to yourselves in psalms and hymns and spiritual songs, singing and making melody in your heart to the Lord.

EPHESIANS 5:19

▌ Thanksgiving and Worship
Giving thanks always for all things unto God and the Father in the name of our Lord Jesus Christ.

EPHESIANS 5:20

▌ Thirsty for more
If any man thirst, let him come unto me, and drink. He that believeth on me, as the scripture hath said, out of his belly shall flow rivers of living water.

JOHN 7:37-38

I thirst for more! Are you thirsty for more of his refilling, strength and refreshing? I keep myself refilled or continuously filled and refreshed with the Spirit by praying and praising in tongues regularly. Worshiping God is amazing! I enjoy worshiping God by myself, loving on Him and thanking Him. I find myself refreshed after spending time in His presence and so will you!

8 BE CONSISTENT

The secret to winning is to be consistent. Anything that you stay consistent with will break through for you. Inconsistency saps your good intentions of the desired results. Without consistency in life, dreams look as far away as the horizon and desires are denied. When you are consistent, it enables you to make great strides in your chosen field. Everyone knows someone who started to go to the gym and pay a monthly fee, only to go for one month and give up after that. This is why their physique has not changed. The intention was there but the consistency was not. It is through consistency that you will see the fruit of your labor. Being consistent simply means that you do not quit even when you feel like it, but you press through to the other side. Consistency brings that – which is far off – into our hands as living realities. As you pursue the journey of developing a strong spirit, keep on your quest, knowing that God will back you up all the way.

CHAPTER 10
BUILDING A STRONG SPIRIT THROUGH 'REDEMPTION CONFESSION'

Take with you words, and turn to the LORD: say unto him, Take away all iniquity, and receive us graciously: so will we render the calves of our lips.
HEBREWS 14:2

Take words with you and return to the LORD. Say to Him, "Take away all iniquity And receive us graciously, That we may present the fruit of our lips."
NASB

Prepare your confession and come back to God. Pray to him, 'Take away our sin, accept our confession. Receive as restitution our repentant prayers.
MESSAGE BIBLE

You cannot separate Christianity from confession. Whether it is confessing Jesus Christ as your Lord, confession of sins or confession of your position in Christ, you simply cannot take confession away from Christianity. Christianity was known as the great confession and indeed it is. Christianity and confession are inseparable. In Christianity, you have the **initial confession** that immersed you into the body of Christ and you have the **continual confession** that immerses the Word of Christ into your spirit, mind and body. As I mentioned earlier, the **initial confession** declared the Lordship of Christ over your life but the **continual confession** declares your mastery in Christ over the world, the flesh and the devil. Once you grasp this revelation, you will be more careful about how you speak concerning yourself and circumstances.

You must understand that the abiding Word is the secret to answered prayer. Here is how Jesus put it:

If ye abide in me, and my words abide in you, ye shall ask what ye will, and it shall be done unto you.

JOHN 15:7

Christianity and confession are inseparable

The confessing of the Word will be the building of your faith and the edifying of your being. Keep in mind that Jesus is the apostle and high priest of your confession (Hebrews 3:1). This means that as an apostle He is a sent, or commissioned one, to offer your sacrifices of words before the throne of God. This is why Hosea said, 'Take with you words' or as The Message Bible aptly pens it, 'Prepare your confession... receive as restitution...'. Your confession will bring restitution to your life.

Restitution simply means:

❖ The restoration of something lost or stolen to its proper owner;
❖ The restoration of something to its original state.

This is why it is important for you to bring the fruit of the lips as sacrifices for Jesus your High Priest, to take them to the heavenly altar before the Father. Your words matter! Thousands of years ago, King Solomon wisely said: '*Thou art snared with the words of thy mouth, thou art taken with the words of thy mouth.*' (Proverbs 6:2). In fact one version says: '*You are trapped by the words of your mouth.*' Job also uttered this great revelation: '*How forcible are right words...*' (Job 6:25). The wise centurion, of whom Jesus said had the greatest faith in Israel said: '*Speak the Word only and my servant shall be healed*' (Matthew 8:8). The man knew there was healing in Jesus' words. You see words are spiritual forces that have effects upon the physical. Words are containers and carriers that make deliveries.

Words are no respecter of persons, they just make deliveries. This is why we have to prepare our confessions because we want good deliveries to be made to our home address. A prepared confession is one which is based in our redemption. The Scripture is clear on the matter:

> *Let the redeemed of the Lord say so, whom he hath redeemed from the hand of the enemy.*
>
> PSALM 107:2

As believers who endeavor to be strong in spirit and be sustained, we must learn to sustain a 'redemption confession' daily. Redemption will not become a living reality in you until you learn to accept, acknowledge, believe, confess and receive it. Faith is governed by our confession. Your life cannot go any higher than your level of confession. You will rise or fall on your confession. A confession dipped in doubt and unbelief will curtail the work of the Holy Spirit in your life but a bold clear-cut confession like when the Father, in spite of the darkness, said, 'Light be', will cause the Spirit to move from hovering over the waters to creating light. Another bold and clear-cut confession is Paul saying: *'I know in whom I have believed and I am fully persuaded'* (2 Timothy 1:12). God told Jeremiah: *'I will hasten my word to perform it.'* (Jeremiah 1:12). These are the kinds of confessions that God will back up. Once you speak His Word, He hastens to perform them. Your confession is your faith expressed, dominating the world. Your spirit corresponds to your confession, triggering its rise in dominion over the outward elements.

The greatest battle that you will have will be the battle to maintain a good confession in the midst of dire and impossible situations. This is why the author of Hebrews reminded us:

> *Let us hold fast the profession of our faith without wavering...*
>
> HEBREWS 10:23

In other words, the devil and hell will throw everything at you but you must remain unswervingly steadfast in your confession because God always keeps His Word even when all the odds are against it. Don't let the devil take you off your confession of your redemption. Confession will aid you in getting a strong spirit and a strong spirit empowers you in holding fast to your confession of redemption.

9 WHAT ARE WE TO CONFESS

Go through your New Testament and find all the 'in him', 'in whom' and 'in Christ' verses and confess them as your new identification. I will list some of the verses for you:

▶ In Him

*For **in Him** we live and move and have our being...*

ACTS 17:2

*For he hath made him to be sin for us, who knew no sin; that we might be **made the righteousness of God in him**.*

2 CORINTHIANS 5:21

*For **in him** dwelleth all the fulness of the Godhead bodily. And* **ye are complete in him,** *which is the head of all principality and power.*

COLOSSIANS 2:9-10

*Hereby know we that **we dwell in him, and he in us**, because he hath given us of his Spirit.*

1 JOHN 4:13

▶ In whom
In whom we have boldness and access with confidence by the faith of him.

EPHESIANS 3:12

*Giving thanks unto the Father, which hath made us meet to be partakers of the inheritance of the saints in light: Who hath delivered us from the power of darkness, and hath translated us into the kingdom of his dear Son: **In whom we have redemption through his blood,** even the forgiveness of sins.*

COLOSSIANS 1:12-14

In Christ

*Being justified freely by his grace through the **redemption that is in Christ Jesus.***

ROMANS 3:24

*There is therefore now **no condemnation to them which are in Christ Jesus,** who walk not after the flesh, but after the Spirit. For the **law of the Spirit of life in Christ Jesus hath made me free from the law of sin and death.***

ROMANS 8:1-2

*But of him are ye **in Christ Jesus, who of God is made unto us wisdom, and righteousness, and sanctification, and redemption.***

1 CORINTHIANS 1:30

*For as in Adam all die, even so **in Christ shall all be made alive.***

1 CORINTHIANS 15:22

*Now thanks be unto God, which always causeth us to **triumph in Christ,** and maketh manifest the savour of his knowledge by us in every place.*

2 CORINTHIANS 2:14

*Therefore if **any man be in Christ, he is a new creature:** old things are passed away; behold, all things are become new.*

2 CORINTHIANS 5:17

*Blessed be the God and Father of our Lord Jesus Christ, who hath **blessed us with all spiritual blessings in heavenly places in Christ.***

EPHESIANS 1:3

*And raised us up together, and **made us sit together in the heavenly places in Christ** Jesus.*

EPHESIANS 2:6

*For we are his **workmanship, created in Christ Jesus** unto good works, which God hath before ordained that we should walk in them.*

EPHESIANS 2:10

The more you confess these 'in him', 'in whom' and 'in Christ' truths, the more they will be established as your new identity in Christ. The book of Job tells us:'*Thou shalt also decree a thing, and it shall be established unto thee: and the light shall shine upon thy ways. When men are cast down, then thou shalt say, There is lifting up; and he shall save the humble person.*' (Job 22:28-29). So decree boldly your redemptive identity. They and all the other Scriptures reveal the new creation man as God intends for him to live and reign in life. Go through as many verses as possible and make it a part of your daily talk and conversation. The Lord Jesus did say: '*...he shall have whatsoever he saith.*' (Mark 11:23). So say what you want to see as realities in your life. As an example you can implement this in your daily confession:

Jesus Christ is Lord over my life. He is Lord over my spirit, soul and body. I believe in my heart that God raised Him from the dead, and I confess with my mouth that Jesus Christ is Lord of heaven and earth.

I am born again and I am a new creature in Christ Jesus. God is my Father, and I am His child, washed in the blood of Jesus with my name in the Lamb's book of life.

I am born again to reign in life: old things have passed away and all things are new for me. What was passed down from Adam to me has been cut off in Christ. He is the vine and I am the branch. I abide in Him and His Word abides in me.

I have received eternal life, the God kind of life, the super abundant life and the nature of God is in me. I am justified and have received the righteousness of God in my spirit. Therefore I can do all things through Christ who strengthens me.

Greater is He that is in me than he that is in the world. By the blood of Jesus, I overcome all the works of the devil. By His name, I have authority over principalities and powers. By his Word, I have dominion over sickness and disease.

Now thanks be unto God, who always causes me to triumph in Christ and makes manifest the savor of His knowledge by me in every place. I am the redeemed of the Lord. Therefore there is now no condemnation for me in Christ Jesus. I do not walk after the flesh, but after the Spirit.

I cannot be defeated. I will never quit. I am more than a conqueror in Christ Jesus. I have the victory because of Jesus. I am above only and never beneath. I am the head and not the tail.

The Lord blesses my coming in and my going out. I am protected from the scourge of the tongue. I laugh at calamity and destruction because I am seated in heavenly places in Christ Jesus.

I am strong in the Lord, strong in the Word and strong in my spirit. My spirit – by the Holy Spirit – sustains me.

The spirit of a man will sustain his infirmity; but a wounded spirit who can bear?

PROVERBS 18:14

I laid me down and slept; I awaked; for the Lord sustained me. I will not be afraid of ten thousands of people, that have set themselves against me round about.

PSALM 3:5-6

Many there be which say of my soul, There is no help for him in God. Selah. But thou, O Lord, art a shield for me; my glory, and the lifter up of mine head.

PSALM 3:2-3

ABOUT THE AUTHOR

D R. Glenn Arekion is a uniquely gifted teacher and conference speaker. He conveys the Word of Truth in a simple, yet dynamic and motivational, way. With more than two decades' experience, he travels the globe mentoring leaders, equipping businessmen, and ministering to people, helping them to fulfill their purpose in life. He is a captivating and much sought-after speaker.

The author of thirty books, Glenn is dedicated to transforming lives from defeat into victory. His teaching materials are sold in many countries and are popular among those with a desire to grow strong in faith and experience great success.

Glenn is apostolic in his thrust of ministry. He believes in establishing churches, and teaching and training pastors in their calling. His television program, Faithlift, airs twice a week on The Word Network. Faithlift is also a daily television program on the Faithworld Channel in the U.K. and all over Europe.

Born in Mauritius, Africa, but raised and educated in London, Glenn holds a master's degrees and three doctorate degrees.

Glenn and his beautiful wife, Rosanna, have three children – Lisa, Ethan, and Jodie – and reside in Kentucky.

Author Contact

Glenn Arekion Ministries
P.O. Box 197777
Louisville, KY 40259, USA
mail@glennarekion.org
www.glennarekion.org

Further books by Dr Glenn Arekion

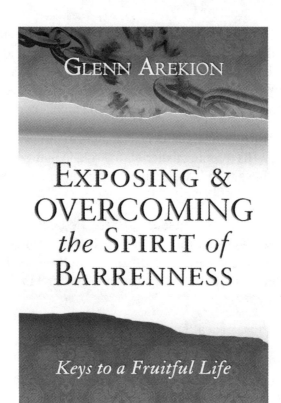

Available online at **glennarekion.org**

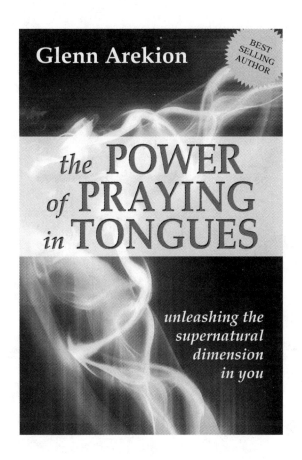

Available online at **glennarekion.org**

Also available in French and Spanish

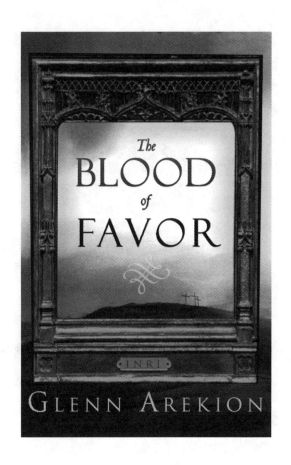

Available online at **glennarekion.org**

Available online at **glennarekion.org**

Available online at **glennarekion.org**

Also available in French

Available online at **glennarekion.org**

GLENN AREKION

TURNING YOUR
DREAMS
INTO REALITIES

Available online at **glennarekion.org**

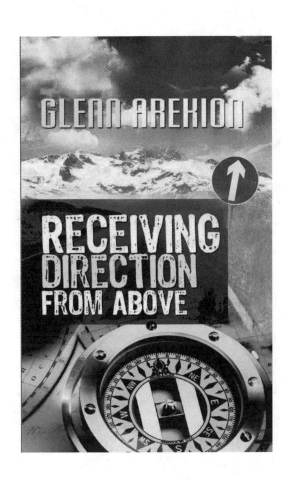

Available online at **glennarekion.org**

Available online at **glennarekion.org**

People Like You... Make People Like Me... Go!

So two good things happen as a result of your gifts—those in need are helped, and they overflow with thanks to God. Those you help will be glad not only because of your generous gifts to themselves and others, but they will praise God for this proof that your deeds are as good as your doctrine. And they will pray for you with deep fervor and feeling because of the wonderful grace of God shown through you
2 Corinthians 9:12-14 – Living Bible

Every major ministry making an impact in the world today is blessed with faithful financial and prayerful partners. Partnership with a ministry is a crucial way for the Gospel to go in all the world. Together, I am totally convinced that we can impact the world and accomplish great things to the glory of God.

I have a simple vision burning in my spirit and that is to unveil the Good News to sinners and saints that victory is available in life through Jesus Christ. Therefore partners are an important part of this ministry and their assistance enable us to accomplish the following:

❖ Globally preach the Gospel through the media: The Word Network;
❖ Travel and preach the Gospel to the nations;
❖ Author books anointed by the Holy Spirit, endowed with information that will radically transform the lives of believers;
❖ Healing crusades and conventions worldwide;
❖ Planting churches in different nations.

Partners help us to do what we cannot do by ourselves.

Not everyone is called to full time ministry but every one is called to reach our world. Everyone who actively participates in supporting Glenn Arekion Ministries with their finances and prayers will receive credit and rewards for whatever this ministry accomplishes.

So join me as a partner today and be part of this end-time harvest! Together, let's reach the millions who need to hear the gospel of Jesus Christ. Your partnership with me will give you the personal satisfaction of being part of a strong ministry who is doing its best to fulfill the Great Commission. You can have the confidence of sowing into a ministry of integrity, knowing that your support is accomplishing the work of the gospel.

Visit **glennarekion.org/support-gam** today and join us!